*Chef/'shef/*n *[F, short for* chef de cuisine
*head of the kitchen] 1: a skilled male cook who
manages a kitchen.*

WOMEN CHEFS

*A Collection of Portraits and Recipes
from California's Culinary Pioneers*

JIM BURNS *and* BETTY ANN BROWN

Introduction by MADELEINE KAMMAN

ARIS BOOKS   BERKELEY   CALIFORNIA

LIBRARY OF CONGRESS CATALOGING-IN-PUBLICATION DATA
Burns, Jim, 1952–
    Women chefs.
    Includes index.
    1. Cookery, American—California style. 2. Women cooks—California—Biography. 3. Cooks—California—Biography. I. Brown, Betty Ann. II. Title.
TX715.B958   1987   641.59794   87-19453
ISBN 0-943186-37-4

Aris Books are published by
Harris Publishing Company, Inc.
1621 Fifth Street, Berkeley, CA 94710
(415) 527-5171

Cover painting by DENISE DUBROY
Design and typography by WILSTED & TAYLOR
Text and recipes edited by FRANCES BOWLES
Recipe testing and consultation by AMARYLL SCHWERTNER

First printing: October, 1987
10 9 8 7 6 5 4 3 2

We dedicate this book to our son,
William James Brown Burns, age 3,
who has sat through his fair share of interviews,
more or less without complaint.

CONTENTS

MISCELLANY

LIST OF THE RECIPES

FOREWORD

BY LOIS DWAN

*Free-lance Food Writer & Former Restaurant Critic
for the* Los Angeles Times

WHENEVER my German grandmother prepared dinner for her assembled family—far too many ever to fit around a single table—the men were served first, then the children and, finally, the weary women. They came in from the kitchen to the crumbs and muss and nibbled listlessly while the men settled contentedly over cigars in another room. Even as a child and long before the siren winds of women's lib, I found this monstrously unfair. It was not all that work I resented, but the taking-for-grantedness.

My mother accepted no such order. Once dinner was served, the door was closed firmly and finally on her kitchen self. She wore another dress to the table over which she presided. Children cleared and washed the dishes. She did not, however, question her obligation to plan and prepare the meal. Indeed, she liked to cook and did it well. She simply made it clear that there was more to her life than that.

I, too, liked to cook and I, too, accepted the obligation—even found pleasure in it—for a while; until the mistral uneasiness abroad in the land blew my way, eroding obligations and rousing old dreams. When my generation came out of the kitchen, we slammed the door and locked it.

Now, with what would have been considered natural perversity in my grandmother's day, women are beating on that same door, trying as hard to get in as they once tried to get out—and finding it as difficult. It *is* a little perverse. The professional kitchen has as much drudgery in it as the home

XIII

kitchen and considerably more tension. Possibly, this almost-last barricade would never have been stormed if fine food and fine restaurants had not become so vital a part of our living.

Cooking as a creative challenge is quite different from cooking as an obligation. The chef becomes not only a respected professional but also a celebrity, with an income risen to Mercedes heights. Naturally, women are as attracted to this transformed world of the kitchen as are men. Good chefs are still in short supply, but men have not been welcoming women into their professional kitchens—for all the irrational reasons that once decreed a kitchen their natural habitat: women are not strong enough; women are emotional; women can't take the pressure.

An Italian chef had his own theory: It is in a woman's nature to cook, therefore she has no need to learn; but, because cooking is not natural to a man, he must study and practice. Therefore, he becomes an *intellectual* chef, concerned with theories and complexities, whereas she remains an *instinctive* cook, a primitive. Of course, he admitted—a little wistfully, I thought—that her cooking can also be very good, the food of the heart, the food we love. But it will not be the food of the mind.

I did not have enough Italian to ask how they would compare as chefs if woman's natural ability were disciplined in the same manner as man's unnatural ability.

Jim Burns and Betty Ann Brown have gathered together the stories of the women chefs who have made it over the barriers to reach a degree of recognition in California. They have charted the chefs' progress in this unnatural battle, related their experiences, their failures, and their successes. The stories have been both similar and different. Some chefs grow their own produce in country towns. Some cope in cities. Some have husbands to help and encourage. Some are alone with experienced or inexperienced help. Some are young and some not so. Some cook with their minds as well as with their hearts.

The result is a fascinating chronicle of a particular time and place in our history, one more facet—possibly one of the strangest—of woman's struggle to find where she best belongs.

ACKNOWLEDGMENTS

WE THANK Lois Dwan, Julia Child, Sheila Lowenstein, Sara Moulton, Barbara Wheaton, Barbara Haber, Madeleine Kamman, Sonia Landes, Larry Pryor, Ruth Reichl, Nick Walker, Fenton and Nancy Jones, Dolores Pacileo, David Thomson, Michael Wild, Sylvie C. Brown, Kelyn Roberts, Amaryll Schwertner, and Frances Bowles for all their help. And a special thanks to John Harris, our publisher, for all his enthusiastic support and creative input.

INTRODUCTION

BY MADELEINE KAMMAN

SHE STOOD FIVE FEET TALL, with a bit of a sharp nose and very dark bright eyes. Her chestnut brown hair was pulled back just enough to make her appear grand rather than severe. Her name was not embroidered on her kitchen whites. In those days no woman, and no man for that matter, would have dreamed of ever doing something so forward. She was modest, capable, totally professional. To her I owe my knowledge of kitchen procedures; I still teach her methods. Her name was Claire Robert. She was my great-aunt and a great chef. She died in 1955, passing on to me a legacy, which, if she were to know how far it reached, would have left her puzzled.

I landed in Philadelphia in early 1961, the first of my family ever to emigrate and a bit shaky at having left my country behind. I was made of nine hundred years of French blood. I started cooking up a storm to sublimate my homesickness. My visits to local restaurants were disappointing, monotonous, uninspiring. One restaurant owner asked me to help try to remedy the situation. I produced for him a wonderful little kitchen manual for a fee of $100. His chef threw it away, telling him that I, as a woman, "really did not know the score." I tucked my own copy away; it was not to be a total loss.

By the time I reached Boston in 1969, I had started writing my first book, *The Making of a Cook*. My second child was three years old and it was in his cheerful company that I finished writing the book. I gave him my three percolators all in pieces and, by the time I had written for an hour, he had put them back together. Then we both paused for Oreos and milk and started all over again, he reassembling coffee pots and I writing.

The book was finished and published as my Boston cooking school opened. It took me exactly two weeks to realize that the school would never work financially unless it generated a steady income. The restaurant situation in Boston being no better than it had been in Philadelphia, I decided to offer a professional chefs' training program. Dr. Rachel K. Weiner of the Massachusetts Board of Education understood right away that I would be providing a solid education and licensed the school. As it turned out, she was the only woman in Boston who would ever be helpful; any other help was to come, directly or indirectly, from men.

As early as 1971, we started serving meals on a part-time basis. Economics pushed us onward. Three students sent by the Massachusetts Rehabilitation Program dropped out and with them went the rent for the summer of 1975. The graduates of the chefs' training program were looking for work and I was looking for money. This is when I pulled out that small kitchen manual written a few years before and, within a week, we had a restaurant on the premises of the school. That it was a relatively rapid success was due in part to the big heart of Anthony Spinazzola, then the food critic for the *Boston Globe*, who wrote the nicest article after our opening dinner, and in part to my iron hand guiding a bunch of wonderful—oh so wonderful—kids who were going to become some of the best cooking teachers and chefs in the United States. Imagine, however, trying to establish yourself as a woman chef in 1975 with a strong feminist movement clamoring that women had to get out of the kitchen and Paul Bocuse declaring in *Newsweek* that there was no place for women in professional kitchens, that they belonged "in bed." I decided to exploit that statement and hang upside down a framed and signed menu he had given me in which he had—should I say imprudently—written: "To Madeleine Kamman, the best restaurant in the United States." Of course it created a stir as every reviewer asked why I hung that august person's testimonial upside down. But, it was really the quality of the offerings that tipped the scale.

The country at large gave us a lot of support as people from all over America, and even Europe flooded our dining room on the weekends. To survive economically on weekdays, I had to create inexpensive menus: Boston itself was not ready for us yet. No little vegetables were available then. You worked with whatever greens you had and it was up to you to present them in different ways. Mussels and Belon oysters came from that other pioneer, Mr. Ed Meyers, in Walpole, Maine; the truffles were flown in fresh from France during the winter, and the *foie gras* was canned, *demi-cuit*, for me each Monday in the Landes to be served on Friday and Saturday night of that week. What a wonderful experience! I was on a constant high. I loved it, even if it meant involving my children in the project so that I could keep my eyes on them or getting up at 3:30 A.M. to grind *terrines*. The fatigue was immense, not only for me. I distinctly remember Jimmy Schmidt sitting on the floor after a frantic evening, dripping wet, his baseball cap askew on his blond hair.

There is no doubt that I became extremely controversial. I knew it, but I persisted in being so because, deep down, I was aware that I was doing something that would pave the way for the generation of women immediately following me. What a pleasure to see Lydia Shire write that she "never felt discriminated against as a woman." I did, and seriously so. I had endless difficulties securing bank loans. I was refused membership in the Escoffier Society of Boston because I was a woman and told to join the Ladies of Escoffier. I never did and never will. I even left the French Association des Restauratrices Cuisinières because I realized one day that a culinary professional association is valid only when both sexes are represented equally.

This new book on California's women chefs is welcome. It presents a diverse and interesting collection of women and their stories and recipes from one of America's most productive culinary regions. I wish it could cover all of the United States so as to recognize the many who have worked very hard all over the country. I know that other volumes will follow this one. I would like to mention that the true pioneers in California and those with whom I feel the greatest kinship are my compatriot, Josephine Araldo, who, at the age of ninety, still imparts her knowledge, the brilliant Joyce Goldstein who, I know, will continue meeting with success, the serene Marion Cunningham who modernized Fannie Farmer for us and, of course, Alice Waters, who is by now an institution.

Women have been penalized for centuries by being called "just cooks." It is utterly unfair considering that, in my opinion, they work twice as hard as men chefs do. Many women chefs have raised their own children and educated those of other men and women in kitchen work for centuries while running profitable businesses and so deserving the title of chef. Guégan, in *Le Cuisinier Français*, specifically mentions several seventeenth-century women whose *cabarets* were good enough for very important people to support them.

Right now, I feel that the only difference between Escoffier and myself is that he was lucky enough to capture the attention of Cesar Ritz. Many women nowadays are finding their own Ritz and it is a good feeling to know that many more will. One day one of the young women I trained said to me: "I am a feminist but I am not as loud as you were." To which I responded, "I had to be loud, to make sure that your generation would never have to be." The work is by no means finished but it will be soon. The best of luck to those who are still on their way to success.

WOMEN CHEFS

A WOMAN'S PLACE

IN RESTAURANT REVIEWS, magazine articles, and popular food books, you can see the beginnings of a revolution—the rise of women chefs. For the first time in history significant numbers of women are cooking in top restaurants, and are getting credit for it. Although the phenomenon is nationwide, this book concentrates on some of the talented women chefs who work in California, home of California cuisine. Just as a lack of vested traditionalism allowed room for experimentation and the invention of a new way of cooking, so too it allowed for gender reshuffling in the kitchen. The story begins, however, in France, where the modern restaurant originated.

The history of the French food business starts with the medieval guilds, the antecedents of our modern labor unions. There were guilds for butchers, for bakers, for pastry chefs. Training for and admission to each profession was rigidly controlled by guild regulations. According to *The New Larousse Gastronomique*:

> In France, a butchers' guild had been established by the eighth century; a man had to serve three years' apprenticeship and buy, dress, cut, and sell meat for a further three years before he could become a master butcher and buy an official diploma; both privileges cost a great deal of money. The guild was directed by a master of master butchers, and became extremely powerful, arrogating to themselves not only the monopoly of selling beef, veal, mutton, pork, and sucking-pig, but also sea and river fish.
>
> Charles VI revoked some of their privileges, and their power declined for a time, but in the sixteenth century, they were raised to

the status of tradesmen, and were subject to statutes, among which were ordinances which forbade them to open new stalls without authority; keep open after a certain time . . . solicit custom or abuse customers . . . sell cooked meat; or pursue any other trade but that of a butcher. . . . The royal regulations were maintained until the end of absolute monarchy [New York: Crown, 1977, page 765].

One way in which to circumvent the costs of guild admission (and also perhaps to avoid some of the gruelling work involved) was to be the son of a master craftsman. *Larousse* tells us, for example, that for bakers, the "apprenticeships lasted five years, followed by four years working for the bakers' guild. At the end of the nine years, the apprentice, *unless he was the master baker's son* (italics added) had to present his *chef d'oeuvre* and, on paying for a certificate, might at last practice as a master baker [ibid.]."

French women, who were by law prohibited from owning most property, could rarely afford to buy their way into the guilds' training systems. Property laws also forbade, in most circumstances, their inheritance of family businesses. They could never be the master baker's "son." (There were exceptions: Women sometimes took over their fathers' positions in the guilds controlling fine arts production. For example, Sabina von Steinbach continued her father's work on the sculptural façade of the Strasbourg Cathedral.) Social conventions reinforced the legal restrictions: we haven't found any record of a French woman in the food guilds before the twentieth century.

In the mid-eighteenth century, the traveller to Paris had only a few options for a meal outside a private home or palace. According to Brillat-Savarin, in his *Physiology of Taste*, such a traveller would be

forced to have recourse to the fare provided at his inn, which was usually bad. There were one or two hotels boasting a *table d'hôte* . . . which, however, with few exceptions offered none but the barest necessaries, and could only be had at a stated hour.

He had, it is true, caterers to fall back on; but they only supplied complete meals, and whoever wished to entertain a few friends was obliged to order his requirements in advance; so that the visitor who had not the good fortune to be invited to some wealthy house would leave our great city in total ignorance of the resources and delights of French cookery [New Haven, Conn.: Leete's Island, 1977, page 227].

A soup vendor named Boulanger changed all that. In 1765, the sign over his establishment read: "*Venite ad me omnes qui stomacho laboratis et ego restaurabo vos.*" (Come to me all ye whose stomachs suffer and I will restore you.) Boulanger offered his fare throughout the day and into the evening. He allowed his patrons to select from a menu. One dish he served—sheep's feet in white wine sauce—caused quite a stir. At that time, only *traiteurs* (caterers) were allowed to serve whole pieces of meat or fowl and *ragoûts*. Since Boulanger, who was not a member of the *traiteurs'* guild, was apparently serving a *ragoût*, he must be breaking the law. The *traiteurs* took him to court. The judges ruled in Boulanger's favor, holding that his sheep's feet creation was not a *ragoût* and, therefore, not illegal for sale to the public. They had ruled in favor of the forerunner of the modern restaurant.

The restaurant differed from all its predecessors. The customer could choose what he wanted from a menu, know each item's price, order practically whenever he wanted to, and enjoy his meal on the premises. The exciting new form of food venture attracted many diverse entrepreneurs, and after the Revolution of 1789, a great number of chefs who were forced to leave the aristocrats' payrolls opened their own restaurants. A new profession was born.

A record of the better French restaurants from the late eighteenth century until the Second World War is given in *Larousse Gastronomique* under the heading "Restaurants of Bygone Days." Of the sixty-two establishments listed, only five were associated with women, two of whom are described as "excellent cooks"; none is referred to as a "chef," an appellation given most of the fifty-seven men discussed. The terms *cook* and *chef* are not interchangeable. Only when a cook has training, respect, and responsibility does she become a chef. Cooks work in homes or in diners; chefs work in restaurants. Is it possible that Larousse's two women—Mère Saguet and Madame Prunier—were chefs whose historical record has been distorted, however inadvertently, by sexism in labelling, or practice, or both? French male chefs have a history of objecting to their female counterparts on three points. They hold that women are weak, that they are disruptive in the kitchen, that they have inferior sensibilities.

Certainly, the nineteenth-century kitchen portrayed by Marie-Antoine Carême, the founder of classic French cooking, shows how demanding the place could be.

> Imagine yourself in a large kitchen such as that of the Foreign Ministry at the moment of a great dinner. Twenty chefs are at their occupations, coming, going, moving with speed at this cauldron of heat. Look at that great mass of live charcoal . . . .
>
> Add to that a heap of burning wood in front of which four spits are turning, one of which bears a sirloin weighing twenty to twenty-seven kilograms . . . only the chef has the right to make himself heard, and at the sound of his voice everyone obeys . . . for about half an hour the doors and windows are closed so that the air does not cool the dishes as they are being dished up . . . . But it is the burning charcoal which kills us [*Larousse*, page 271].

Paul Bocuse, best known of the *nouvelle cuisine* chefs, rekindled the debate some years ago when he said over French radio that women were "too weak" to lift the heavy kitchen pots, called *marmites*. In response not to Bocuse, but to the issue of women's physical weakness, Julia Child said, "I don't buy that nonsense that women can't lift heavy pots. There are always plenty of people around to help." The fact that there are other styles of kitchen preparation also deflates Bocuse's allegation. Madame Trama, chef and proprietor of Tante Madée restaurant in Paris, said, "I don't need big marmites. I make my dishes in little copper pots—to order." The tradition of women running smaller kitchens in the French countryside is well documented. The French provincial and regional cuisines, sometimes called *cuisine de terroir, cuisine de misère*, or even *cuisine des femmes*, were heavily influenced by the *mères cuisinières*.

The second allegation is that women will be sexually disruptive in the kitchen. Georgette Descat's son, who is business manager of her Lous Landes restaurant in Paris, while being interviewed for an article about women chefs, repeated what he had heard male chefs say about their female counterparts: "They'll throw the place in an uproar. The men will feel them up (*les fureter*) and jump them on the piano [slang for stove]. The big chefs don't say they won't hire a woman, but the fact is they don't."

One woman chef currently working in Los Angeles had to deal with sexual harassment during her apprenticeship in Michel Guérard's kitchen. One of the other apprentices, whom she nicknamed "The Breather," began panting loudly and staring at her every time she entered the kitchen. Neither his superiors nor his co-workers reprimanded him.

The last criticism of women as potential chefs is the most absurd. In his *Gold Cook Book*, published in 1947, Louis P. De Gouy, a master chef, wrote:

> Despite all the arguments to the contrary, men, in general, seem to
> have a keener sense of smell than women (though it is admitted that
> men are greatly inferior in some of the other human qualities!);
> they have a true gustatory tongue for flavor—one of the reasons
> that men exclusively are engaged in wine, tea, and coffee tasting.
> They make, therefore, the best chefs [New York: Chilton, 1947,
> page 557].

De Gouy's statement seems too ridiculous to merit response, but it unfortunately expresses a sentiment shared by other male chefs: women are felt to be innately inferior when it comes to cooking.

To fight back against this kind of chauvinism in the professional kitchen, French women started an organization to help themselves. As writer Sonia Landes explains in *The New Boston Review*, "When Annie Desvignes, a restauratrice in Vervins, was refused admission into the Society of Chefs because she was a woman, she called her good friend and friend of women chefs, Robert Courtine, for help. Courtine, better known as La Reynière, is the influential food writer for *Le Monde*."

Courtine addressed Desvignes' plight directly in his newspaper column. In an open letter he wrote, "Why do you need the company of men to discuss cuisine? Form your own association." That is exactly what happened on December 20, 1975, at Ty-Coz, a Parisian restaurant. Six women chefs met, and the Association des Restauratrices-Cuisinières emerged. From that small core the group has grown to include chefs from fifty-nine establishments. Each member chef is also the owner of her restaurant. Few of the members work outside France. As the years passed, Courtine still seems enamoured with the group. In his introduction to its latest directory he wrote, "These women cook like a bird sings."

More recently in the United States the Los Angeles Women's Culinary Alliance was formed by a group of young professional chefs. The organization was not formed in response to sexism or bias, but because the founders felt that there was a real need for an organization that would provide a sense of community for women in the food profession. There are currently 150 members.

Early in this country's history the food for those who could afford fine dining came directly from the French tradition of *grande cuisine*. A French chef was a status symbol for the wealthy. When Thomas Jefferson became president he hired a French chef for the White House. Significantly, he also "brought in two black women to apprentice with the master and to learn his techniques."

The situation in the Jefferson White House, although more elaborate, was not unlike the way the rest of the wealthy lived. The obligation of cooking was primarily a chore for the domestic servants. Barbara Wheaton, a culinary historian, writes that, "even a modest household might have hired a girl to help. In the idealized world of Louisa May Alcott's *Little Women*, the faithful Hanna Mullett has served the March family since the birth of the oldest son. . . . She washes and irons, cooks, and tends the children. Much of the food charitably taken by the family to the sick and needy is prepared by her ["The Cooks of Concord," *The Journal of Gastronomy*, I, Fall 1984, page 12]." Besides providing the meals at home, women operated and cooked for many of the boarding houses that thrived during the last century. Wheaton notes that Mrs. Thoreau, Henry's mother, was a celebrated cook who ran a number of successful boarding houses.

For the most part, the women who were paid to be America's cooks are historically invisible. There is one instance of a well-known Southern cook auctioning off her services: In 1850, Mammy Pleasant sold her skills for a whopping $500 per month in San Francisco, a city burning with gold fever. Mrs. Thoreau and Mammy Pleasant are the exceptions, however. There are no books on the subject of early American women cooks; those who should be given credit remain nameless.

But while paid servants and boarding house cooks are lost in the anonymity of history, cookbooks provide a substantial record of women's participation in this country's culinary history. The list of cookbooks written by women is long: among them, one can cite: *American Cookery* (1796) by Amelia Simmons, *Mrs. Putnam's Receipt Book* (1856), *The Quickest Guide to Breakfast, Dinner and Supper* (1890) by Aunt Gertrude, and the famous *Boston Cooking School Cook Book*, written by Fannie Farmer in 1896. Women also wrote cookbooks for numerous voluntary associations. The bibliography, *California in the Kitchen*, records the efforts of many church groups, clubs, and auxiliaries over more than a century.

During the late sixties, a number of recent college graduates went to France to learn cooking techniques and then returned to America to work for someone else, or to open their own restaurants. A new generation was ready to take over the professional kitchen. They were well-educated, young, experimental, and free from the conventions of the past. Actually, there were few conventions to hold onto—there never was a guild system in America and the feminist movement had shaken the assumptions about accepted behavior according to gender. The new restaurant could easily accommodate men and women in its kitchen. In a sense, both were pioneers.

Easily the most recognized California women chef and one of the most brilliant names to come out of that vanguard was Alice Waters. Waters says she has always loved the French way of life, that she tried to be "as French as possible." She studied French literature at the University of California at Berkeley. Then she started teaching at a Montessori school, and, with some friends, shared the dream of opening a small, neighborhood restaurant "like those little one-stars in France." That small, neighborhood restaurant became Chez Panisse, which is now internationally famous. The restaurant and indeed California cuisine was based on the inventive use of local, very fresh, and increasingly exotic, produce, along with grilling and lightened sauces. Waters has since opened two other restaurants including one, named for her daughter, Café Fanny.

It was the birth of her daughter Fanny that brought Alice up against one of the central issues for women in the food profession. In a lengthy interview in 1986, she told us that she had delayed having a baby for many years for fear that her work would suffer.

> There are some people who are superhuman and are somehow able to take time for their work, their children, and get everything else done as well. I'm just not that way. I'm scattered enough that when I have the distraction of a little child I can't think clearly about what I'm working on. I can take tastes and make comments at the restaurant, but, for now, I have to rely upon my partners to supply the thoroughness in approach that Chez Panisse has always had.

Whether the issue raised is about having babies, lifting stockpots, or the ability to taste and smell, the fact is that talented women have finally put these obstacles behind them.

The Old World attitude that women can't cook professionally is waning in America. True, when one of the women featured in this book applied for a kitchen job she was offered the post of hatcheck girl instead. True, one woman chef currently working in Los Angeles was doused with cold water thrown from a skylight by a Frenchman who didn't like working with women. But there is a growing number of tally marks in their favor. In 1987, in New York, Anne Rosenzweig, a chef, is orchestrating the renovation of the famous 21 Club; on the West Coast, Lydia Shire, as executive chef, controls the culinary inspiration as well as the kitchens of the Four Seasons, a large hotel in Los Angeles; in Europe, the female *chef-patron* of the Auberge du Père Bise has regained a three-star rating for the restaurant from *Michelin*—who it seems last recognized a woman chef with its three-star accolade in the nineteen fifties, when Mère Brazier in Lyon was honored. In London, the *Sunday Times* named Vivian Abady its Chef of the Year. As Joseph Baum, creator of two highly successful restaurants in New York, the Four Seasons and Windows on the World, told William Rice, the food and wine columnist of *The Chicago Tribune* (and whose essay on women chefs is reprinted here on page 190), "What Anne [Rosenzweig] and Lydia [Shire] are doing represents a new dimension, a change in scale. Their success will mean all the barriers will be down." This book is a celebration of the successes of women chefs in California and, indeed, throughout America.

THE RECIPES

BY AMARYLL SCHWERTNER

WHEN PRESENTED with the task of reducing the great collection of recipes submitted for this book by so many chefs, I chose two general criteria in the hope that these would yield the best representation of each chef's work as evidenced in their restaurants and careers and in their relationships to one another.

Initially I read all of the recipes within the context of the writers' statements and inferred a lot of information about the women and their work simply from their own choice of recipes sent in for consideration. Then, relying on my own personal and professional relationships with many of the chefs and my first-hand experiences in some of the restaurants, I narrowed down the choices. Then followed extensive, random testing. These are all recipes from professional chefs whose manner of working is vastly different from the way one cooks at home (a difference pointed out frequently by the chefs themselves: no one vaulted easily into running a restaurant or a catering business or indeed any professional association with food simply because she was a good cook). I tested the more complex recipes—a gratifying exercise—to ensure that they worked and so that I could present a large variety of ingredients and ideas without too much overlap.

I would like to encourage the readers, in preparing these recipes, to rely particularly on the quality of their ingredients, and then on their own tastes, experiences, and instincts. Those are the considerations by which the dishes were created, the considerations that make each chef's work individual, and the considerations that will produce food that is successful in itself and evocative of the chefs who are portrayed here.

Cindy Black

CINDY BLACK
VICORP SPECIALTY RESTAURANTS, INC.
SAN DIEGO

CINDY BLACK'S SUCCESS in the restaurant field is substantial: She is currently executive chef for all of the eighty-six restaurants owned, across the country, by Vicorp Specialty Restaurants, Inc., a company based in San Diego. The major culinary figure in Cindy's life is not Julia Child, Craig Claiborne, or Paula Wolfert. It's her father, a man who spent his days working for the Foreign Service and his nights refining gustatory experiments. Richard Black gave his daughter a love for food.

At two o'clock in the morning the lights would be on in the Blacks' kitchen. As her father manipulated a stubborn puff pastry around a *pâté*, Cindy would keep him company. When Richard became "le saucier" he would quiz her on the sauce he was constructing and how the ingredients fit together.

After retiring from the Foreign Service, he attended Madeleine Kamman's cooking school, Modern Gourmet. It wasn't long before his daughter was also taking classes. Cindy worked in Madeleine's restaurant, Chez La Mère Madeleine, in New Hampshire, while she finished a degree in French Literature from Wellesley. Madeleine later suggested that Cindy serve her apprenticeship at a friend's restaurant in the southwest of France. Cindy worked as *aide-cuisinière* under Madame Françoise Hanff at Le Cabanon outside Magescq in the Landes region.

"Il faut donner aux gens ce qu'ils aiment," was Madame Hanff's motto; "Give the people what they want." She thought *nouvelle cuisine* was ridiculous. With her rich *cassoulets* and outstanding *confits*, she favored a cooking that was traditional and authentic. Hanff, a strict Roman Catholic, was always modest about her dishes. She stressed that Le Cabanon was not a grand restaurant, like the two-star place close by in Magescq. The Hanff clan did not want to be superstars, a fact that impressed Cindy. She describes their food as "warm, receptive, generous," qualities she strives for in her own cooking.

After more than a year in France, she returned to Boston, looking for work. She answered a blind advertisement that was offering a position with a "new, first-class restaurant." To her surprise, the restaurant was Apley's, in the Sheraton Hotel in Boston. Apley's was the Sheraton Corporation's first attempt to resurrect the fine hotel dining room. While being interviewed, Cindy met the chef, Bob Brady, and liked him because "he didn't seem like an authoritarian." (The two married in the fall of 1984.) Bob had to battle the executive chef of Apley's who didn't want to hire Cindy because "they already had one woman." He relented and she began work in the kitchen as one of eighty chefs. She worked the *garde-manger* station, making terrines, *pâtes*, pastries, and soufflés. After fifteen months there, Cindy decided she wanted to do something on her own. "Apley's was Bob's menu. I wasn't going to advance and be the chef of that restaurant. It didn't seem that I was going anywhere."

Her father, in the meantime, had discovered a new restaurant on Cape Cod. The chef was leaving. Did Cindy want to come up? She took charge of the Cranberry Moose, a restaurant seating seventy-two guests. It was a change from Boston and the immense kitchen at Apley's. "Running a place for the first time isn't exactly the easiest thing in the world," she says. As the season dwindled and the tourists left the beaches and boats, Cindy was approached again by the Sheraton Corporation, about to open another first-class restaurant, this one in San Diego, California. Did she want to be chef?

Sheppard's, the voice on the telephone assured her, was in the early planning stages. A trip to San Diego and a look at the menu made her doubt if she should leave Cape Cod. "In a corporation," she says, "you have a million executives all wanting their personal loves on the menu." Sheppard's first tentative menu included banana-oreo cheesecake, steak tartare, smoked prime rib, and *paella*. By the fourth revision of the menu, she had winnowed out every item she didn't like. The results were gratifying. Sheppard's, said the writer of an article published in *San Diego* magazine about local restaurants, "should also win a prize for finally beating down local prejudice against hotel restaurants. In one year Cindy Black and the Sheppard's staff have managed to impress all skeptics." Cindy is as peripatetic as many women chefs. After Sheppard's, she went to Piret's in Los Angeles, then returned to San Diego to work for Vicorp.

 POTTED CHICKEN LIVERS

I used to make this for my father at home. It's an easy, spreadable pâté *that's good with apéritifs.*

½ pound bacon cubes, minced
1 red onion, minced
1 tablespoon fresh thyme, finely chopped
½ pound ground fresh pork
1 pound cleaned chicken livers
Salt and pepper
2 bay leaves

Sauté the bacon until just golden. Add the onion, thyme, and pork and continue to sauté until the pork is cooked and the onions limp, approximately 5 minutes. Add the chicken livers and cook only until they are still fairly rare in the middle; the residual heat continues to cook them even when the pan is off the flame. (The *pâté* should be pink when it is cool.) Add salt and pepper to taste.

Mince the mixture quite fine and pack it into 4 small (3-inch) crocks or one larger one. Cover with bay leaves and a thin layer of melted fat, lard, or clarified butter to keep the *pâté* from oxidizing. Place in the refrigerator overnight, but serve at room temperature.

MUSSEL BISQUE WITH FRESH PEAS

A recipe created to take full advantage of the beautiful mussels we had at the Cranberry Moose. Bonnie, a waitress, brought in the sweetest peas from her father's farm; they added a tremendous flavor to this dish.

20 good-sized Maine or Santa Barbara mussels,
    or 16 New Zealand mussels
2 cups fresh shucked peas, cooked
$\frac{1}{2}$ cup shallots
1 tablespoon minced garlic
1 whole red onion, sliced
2 bay leaves
2 cups white wine
2 cups good fish stock or clam juice
$\frac{1}{2}$ cup heavy cream
Salt and pepper
Lemon juice to taste
$\frac{1}{2}$ cup snow peas, blanched

Wash the mussels and, along with the peas, shallots, garlic, onion, and bay leaves, steam them open in the wine and stock. Strain the mixture, and reduce the liquid to 3 cups.

Purée 1 cup of the peas (reserving the second cup for the garnish) in a food processor. Add the reduced stock and continue puréeing until smooth. Add the cream. Finish with the lemon juice, salt, and pepper, to taste. Add the mussels, and garnish with sweet and snow peas.

An optional garnish is a dollop of whipped cream, flavored with tomato paste and lemon juice.

CINDY BLACK · 17

PAN-ROASTED ALOUETTES FLAMED IN ARMAGNAC

Alouettes *are tiny larks found in the Landes pine forests. This is an area rich with many varieties of game birds. The hunting season for* alouettes *is very short, therefore in many local restaurants the birds, eaten whole, are sometimes preserved in a sauce and canned for use later in the year.*

1 cup slab bacon, cubed
2 whole, cleaned alouettes *(larks), or substitute 2 or 3*
    quail or 1 squab per person
2 tablespoons dried Provençal herbs (include equal quantities
    of thyme, rosemary, savory, and lavender)
Salt and pepper
4 tablespoons Armagnac

Render the bacon lardons until golden. Drain, set aside the lardons, and leave approximately 2 tablespoons of bacon fat in the pan. Season the birds with the herbs, salt, and pepper and sauté them in the 2 tablespoons of bacon fat until they are evenly brown. Cover the pan and cook slowly, until rich juices have accumulated in the bottom of the pan. If you are cooking *alouettes* or quail, check after 20 minutes; for squab, which should be cooked until medium rare, check after 30 minutes. Return the lardons to the pan, and add the Armagnac and set it alight.

Serve with the pan juices.

ROLLED LOIN OF LAMB WITH CILANTRO

Rolled loin of lamb is sometimes called a boneless English chop. The joint may be roasted whole or divided into individual rounds and sautéed. This dish is especially successful because the apron imparts a good lamb flavor while protecting the loin and tenderloin from losing their juices and becoming overcooked.

Serve with roast peppers and green beans that have been cooked slowly in butter and the lamb juices until they are glazed; this will take about 5 to 10 minutes, during which the lamb will only improve if left to rest in a warm place. Or you may serve the lamb with a potato gratin, the recipe for which follows.

3 pounds whole lamb loin, apron attached, and tenderloin
   reserved
½ cup chopped cilantro
1 tablespoon garlic, finely minced
1 tablespoon fresh thyme, chopped
½ cup fortified wine, preferably port or Madeira
½ cup red wine
4 tablespoons soft butter

Rolled loin of lamb is prepared by boning the loin, butterflying it, and leaving the apron attached. The loin and tenderloin meat should be thoroughly cleaned of any fat and silverskin; the apron cleaned only slightly of fat. Sprinkle the meat with the garlic, thyme, and ¼ cup of the cilantro. Roll up the loin and tenderloin in the apron and portion the lamb into rounds, two per person.

Sauté the lamb rounds over a fairly high heat. They should be cooked brown on the outside and pink in the middle. When the lamb has finished cooking, place the rounds on a platter and keep them warm.

Deglaze the pan with the fortified wine, scraping the brown bits into the sauce. Reduce by half. Add the red wine and reduce again by half. Swirl in the butter, add the rest of the cilantro, and serve.

POTATO GRATIN

6 new red potatoes, thinly sliced
½ cup sliced leeks
2 tablespoons garlic
2 cups heavy cream
1 teaspoon nutmeg
Salt and pepper

In a lightly buttered baking dish, layer the potatoes with the leeks and garlic. Add the cream, seasoned with nutmeg. Bake at approximately 325°F for 1 hour.

 PEACH GRATIN

This is one of my favorite summer desserts.

6 large ripe peaches, peeled and sliced
2 tablespoons lemon juice
1 cup flour
1 cup sugar
¾ cup heavy cream
1 stick plus 2 tablespoons butter
1 egg yolk

Peel the peaches by blanching them for 30 seconds in boiling water. Dip them briefly into cold water and they will be easily peeled.

In a buttered gratin dish, layer the peaches with the lemon juice, a light sprinkling of flour, half a cup of the sugar, and the cream. Build the layers until all the peach slices are used.

Next, make a cookie dough by creaming the stick of butter with the remaining ½ cup of sugar, then add the flour and the egg yolk. Chill the dough in the refrigerator and then roll it out between two sheets of waxed paper. Lay the dough over the peaches and sprinkle with more sugar.

Bake the gratin at 350°F for approximately 45 minutes to 1 hour, until the cookie dough is crisp and golden. (Place a cookie sheet under the gratin dish as the mixture tends to bubble over.) Serve cool, with slightly whipped cream.

Mary Sue Milliken and Susan Feniger

SUSAN FENIGER &
MARY SUE MILLIKEN

CITY RESTAURANT · BORDER GRILL
LOS ANGELES

COULD IT REALLY BE TRUE that once upon a time, after a rainstorm in Paris, two young chefs shook hands under the emerging rainbow and promised that someday they would be their own bosses . . . and that, a few years later, they would be the chefs and owners of the very successful City Restaurant and of the Border Grill, both in Los Angeles? "Yes," affirm Mary Sue Milliken and Susan Feniger, "it's completely true."

"In a year when several important L.A. restaurants opened less formal, less expensive cafés," writes one critic, "the four-year-old City Café turned itself into a hip Mexican restaurant and opened a more formal (though no less hip) restaurant half a mile away." The new 120-seat City Restaurant was created out of a carpet warehouse. It is a *big* place with lots of architectural care taken, but no art on the walls, no flowers on the tables. In an age of the open kitchen, Mary Sue and Susan have gone one better—over the bar there is a TV monitor that offers a constant live view of their kitchen. Knee-deep in flattering reviews of their successful restaurants and cuisine, they are certainly two of the best-trained chef/owners in the country.

Their partnership seems to have been destined from the beginning. They met at Chicago's Le Perroquet. Susan had studied at The Culinary Institute of America, in New York (one of very few women in her class), worked in a fish market, and then with a Swiss chef in Kansas City.

23

Mary Sue started at Chicago's Washburne Trade School, then worked at the Chicago Hilton. There, one afternoon she had to make eighty quarts of hollandaise sauce by hand. She told *California* magazine, "There were times when you couldn't think about how much your arm hurt—you had to make sure your face had the right expression, like you were enjoying it." Next Mary Sue went to Maxim's in Chicago, where the kitchen was so large that the chef called out his orders on a loudspeaker.

While at Maxim's she began her assault on the doors of Le Perroquet, also in Chicago. "When I went to apply, I went all dressed up in my suit, and Jovan [Johann] said, 'I don't have any openings in the kitchen, but do you want to work as the hatcheck girl?'" A year later, when the head chef went on vacation, she and Susan were running the kitchen. "And that was really a shock to Jovan, the owner!"

How did it happen? When Mary Sue did get into the kitchen, she started at the bottom and when she moved to pastries, Susan came in to replace her at peeling shallots. And they followed each other around from station to station. "It was so easy," Susan says, "because we both wanted to learn. We didn't have to get there till eight, but we'd arrive at six and get everything set up." Mary Sue continues, "If we wanted to bone a baby lamb we'd have to go in early to allow for some time when no one else was there. We'd have an idea of how to do it, but you need to try it twenty times to get it right." At Le Perroquet they became really close friends. When Susan moved to Ma Maison, in Los Angeles, and Mary Sue moved to Deerfield to open the Society Café, they kept in touch. Their continued connection was fated. Two weeks before Mary Sue left to work in France she called Susan, only to find out that her friend would be in France at the same time.

Susan went to the south of France and studied with Louis Outhier at L'Oasis in La Napoule. Mary Sue worked in Paris with Dominique Na-mahais in the now-famous Restaurant D'Olympe. "We talked on the phone, crying to each other about how difficult it was, being in a foreign country, the language barrier, the cultural differences."

In the early eighties, Susan was again working at Ma Maison. Every day on her way to work she drove down Melrose Avenue, a street famed for its avant-garde clothiers, funky gift shops, and outrageous punk pretenders. Her route took her past the City Café, a small restaurant whose owners operated the eyeglass business next door. One day, when Susan went in for eyeglasses, they discovered, in casual conversation, that she was a chef. They asked if she had any ideas about a new salad dressing for them. A few months later, she was running the shoebox-sized kitchen. Of course, she called Mary Sue; rainbow promises must be kept.

Today at City Restaurant it has all come true and they have some advice for those thinking of starting their own restaurants. "You better love it, because it's every moment, every spare moment that you have," says Mary Sue. "And you'd better have a lot of stamina because you come up against things in opening a restaurant that you just can't believe," Susan continues, "No matter how well-planned and perfectly ready we thought we were for every possible problem, there were more—more problems with government things and with city things. But we were never thrown off." All the difficulties are worth it, they say. "The rewards are all there, equal to what you spend in emotion and anxiety and hard work . . . and the isolation from your personal or social life. All the sacrifices are worth it, because the rewards are there, too. We would never have done anything else."

 # THAI MELON SALAD

This recipe is derived from a dish Mary Sue discovered in Thailand. The Thais slice up big chunks of melon and dip them into a flavoring that includes ground dried shrimp and cayenne pepper. For this variation, we prepare a small dice of melons and then make a spicy sauce that goes over the top.

3 assorted ripe, colorful melons
3 cloves garlic, puréed
2 tablespoons palm sugar (available from Asian grocers)
¼ cup shrimp sauce (available from Asian grocers)
¼ cup freshly squeezed lemon juice
10 serrano chilies, sliced thinly
1 cup roasted, salted peanuts
½ cup dried shrimp (available from Asian grocers)
1 bunch cilantro

Peel the melons, remove the seeds, and dice into ½-inch squares. Chill until serving time.

Place garlic, sugar, shrimp sauce, lemon juice, and chilies in a bowl and mix thoroughly. Chop the peanuts and shrimp and add to the dressing. Pour the dressing over the melon cubes, and mix in the cilantro. Serve immediately.

NOTE
Palm sugar is a raw sugar that is dense and slightly bitter.

CREAM OF PINTO BEAN SOUP WITH SALSA

We like this soup because of its flavor, of course, but also because of its texture. Puréed thoroughly and then strained, it is very smooth. The crunchy salsa provides an interesting contrast.

1½ cups dried and cleaned pinto beans
2 tablespoons butter
2 yellow onions, diced
4 cups chicken stock
2 cups heavy cream
Salt, pepper, Tabasco sauce, and lemon juice to taste

Bring a large pot of water to the boil, add some salt and the pinto beans. Bring the water back to a boil and simmer for 5 minutes. Drain the beans and, in the same pot, melt the butter. Add the onions and lightly brown them. Add the beans and mix well.

Add the chicken stock and bring to the boil, then simmer till the beans are soft. In a blender, purée the beans with the stock, adding more stock if necessary. Return the soup to the stove and add the heavy cream. Add salt, pepper, Tabasco sauce, and lemon juice to suit your taste. Serve with *Salsa*.

SALSA

6 tomatoes
2 yellow onions
2 to 3 chilies (such as serrano *or* jalapeño; *the number*
 will depend on their hotness; be sure to de-seed them)
1 large bunch cilantro
Salt and freshly ground pepper

Blanch the tomatoes, being extremely careful that they stay firm. Then peel
and seed them in preparation for making *brunoise*, which is a very fine dicing
that you should use on the onions, too.

Chop the chilies and cilantro, also fine. Mix all the *salsa* ingredients together and season to taste. Make it spicy and use as a condiment accom-
panying the soup, not as a garnish in it.

VEGETABLE FRITTERS
WITH CHICKPEA BATTER

This recipe came back with Susan from India. It's a variation on a dish her hosts used to pack for picnic lunches. They would eat the fritters cold, but we prefer to eat them when they are still warm and crispy.

1 cup chickpea flour, sifted
1 cup water
½ teaspoon salt
¼ teaspoon ground turmeric
¼ teaspoon ground cumin
¼ teaspoon ground coriander
1 teaspoon mustard seeds
½ teaspoon poppy seeds
¼ teaspoon cayenne pepper
¼ teaspoon baking powder
½ teaspoon cornstarch
1 teaspoon salad oil

Put the chickpea flour in a bowl. Gradually mix in about ¾ cup of water, until you have a batter thick enough to coat vegetables. Add all the other ingredients and mix well. You may need to add more water to the batter if it gets too thick.

Have ready a variety of vegetables cut into pieces. Broccoli, cauliflower, green onions, bell peppers, squash, mushrooms, and eggplant are all suitable for this recipe. Coat each piece with the batter and fry in deep fat until golden brown. Drain on paper and salt lightly. Soy sauce as well as the following two sauces may be used as dips for the fritters.

YOGHURT SAUCE

1 pint yoghurt
¼ teaspoon salt
¼ teaspoon turmeric
½ teaspoon ground coriander
Pinch hot chili powder
¼ teaspoon paprika

Mix the ingredients together in a bowl.

FRESH GREEN CHUTNEY

1 cup chopped cilantro, packed tightly
½ cup chopped mint, packed tightly
2 cloves garlic, crushed
½ teaspoon salt
1 tablespoon finely grated fresh ginger
1 green chili, finely chopped
Juice of 2 lemons
1 tablespoon olive oil

Mix the ingredients together in a bowl or a food processor.

CONFIT OF DUCK
WITH PARSNIP CHIPS

2 fresh ducks, cleaned
Salt and pepper
5 cups duck fat, or 3 pounds pork fat
10 cloves garlic
1 tablespoon black peppercorns

Remove legs and breasts from the ducks. Season heavily with salt and less heavily with pepper, and leave at room temperature for 45 minutes.

If duck fat is unavailable, rendered pork fat may be used: remove the skin from 3 pounds fatback and cut it in 1-inch cubes. Blanch the cubes in boiling water, drain them, and mince in a food processor. Heat this purée slowly until it is liquified. Strain the liquid into a heavy-bottomed pot.

Add the garlic, peppercorns, and pieces of duck. Cook very, very slowly for 2 hours or more. Test for doneness by piercing the meat with a fork. If the meat falls off the fork easily, remove the pot from the heat and allow the *confit* to cool. The duck may be stored in its own fat for months.

When you're ready to serve it, remove pieces from the fat and scrape off the skin. Place the pieces, in a covered baking dish, in a 350°F oven. When the duck is heated through, the fat will have collected at the bottom of the dish and the meat pieces will be tender and juicy.

PARSNIP CHIPS

1½ pounds parsnips
Oil for deep frying
1 pound clarified butter
Salt

Peel the parsnips and slice them lengthwise, into sticks about ¹⁄₁₆-inch thick. A mandolin is excellent for this, but a very sharp knife and a patient, steady hand will do as well.

Blanch the parsnip slices until they are limp (this takes only moments) in hot oil. Drain and then sauté in clarified butter until they are golden brown and crisp. Drain on paper and salt lightly.

CITY CHOCOLATE WITH ESPRESSO CRÈME ANGLAISE

3 tablespoons brandy
1 cup golden raisins
1 pound, 2 ounces semisweet chocolate
14 ounces sweet butter
10 eggs, separated

Warm the brandy and raisins over a low heat, and leave them to soak while preparing the chocolate. Chop the chocolate into small pieces and melt them, along with the butter, in a double boiler over low heat. When melted, remove immediately, and whisk in the egg yolks and raisins.

Beat the egg whites to soft peaks and fold them into the chocolate mixture. Place it in a 3-cup mold, lined with plastic film, and then aluminum foil. Cover this very full container with plastic film. Chill overnight. Serve the next day with *Espresso Crème Anglaise*.

ESPRESSO CRÈME ANGLAISE

8 egg yolks
9 ounces sugar
2 cups milk
1 tablespoon mocha paste
1 teaspoon vanilla

Beat together the egg yolks and sugar and set aside. Bring the milk to the boil and add the sugar and egg mixture. Return this custard to the heat and cook just until it will coat a spoon. Do not let it boil.

Turn off the heat and add the mocha paste (instant coffee that has been moistened with hot water may be substituted) and the vanilla. Strain through a fine sieve lined with cheesecloth and serve chilled.

SUSAN FENIGER & MARY SUE MILLIKEN · 33

Margaret Fox

MARGARET FOX

CAFÉ BEAUJOLAIS · MENDOCINO

ONE WOULD NEVER IMAGINE that anything runs—or ever ran—less than perfectly in the Victorian-style house, built in 1910, that is the Café Beaujolais. The building is surrounded by trees, vines, and flowers. The backyard view of Mendocino is broad and misty. The interior, furnished with bentwood chairs and heavy oak tables, feels warm, inviting patrons to linger. Yet Café Beaujolais had to struggle to survive. Margaret Fox, who is the chef and owner, bought the restaurant with borrowed money when she was twenty-four years old. She had had no previous restaurant experience, except for nine months spent as a hotel baker. Hers is a story of success through determination and learning along the way.

"I grew up surrounded literally by cookbooks," she says. Her mother had stacks of books on food around the house. Mrs. Fox's collection was not merely a family cook's resource, but also a food library.

Margaret's first job out of college was that of baker at the Mendocino Hotel. She had driven up the California coast with a friend, knocking on doors. By the time they reached Mendocino she was in despair. She stopped at the wine shop to ask if there were any jobs in town. The owner asked her if she could sew. No? "Well, then how about baking?"

Soon, she was in the kitchen of the Mendocino Hotel staring at the biggest Hobart mixer she'd ever seen. It was true that she could bake. It was not true that she had ever baked in a commercial kitchen. She got the job, though: twenty hours a week at $3.25 an hour. Her first batch of bread failed, but she learned to adapt—after some painful adjustment—her recipes from home to the demands of a hotel restaurant.

After nine months, Margaret became restless. "I couldn't stand doing the same thing over and over," she says, although now, in her restaurant, she repeats the same dishes, from the same recipes, many times. She went to another job, but that, too, quickly lost its appeal. In the process Margaret made an important discovery—she needed to work for herself. A restaurant in town was for sale. She walked by, peered through the windows, and managed to convince two friends to pool their money with hers. Together they bought the Café Beaujolais.

She describes the first few months as being much as she would have imagined about owning a restaurant: "It was like a movie! Judy Garland and Mickey Rooney saying, 'Hey, let's have a show!' " As the show went on, the fantasy faded in the hard work and long hours of reality. Her friends thought it was too much.

"I bought everybody out with the help of my parents. They lent me the money. And then it was my baby, and I was nervous, and then slowly it worked. Sometimes I think that the only reason we didn't go out of business was because I made a decision that the only way they would get rid of me would be to physically drag me out of the building."

Not many creditors were willing to do that. She stayed on without enough money to pay the mounting bills, nor enough to hire the help she needed. Margaret decided that, if there were three jobs to be filled and she was the only one who could fill them, she would begin at 5 A.M. and leave the next morning at 1. Upon reflection, Margaret says that the one thing she lacked when she opened Café Beaujolais was not cooking sense, but business sense. Before you try to open a restaurant, she advises, know about the business side, too.

Instead of closing, the restaurant started to succeed. Regular customers filled the gaps left by seasonal tourists. The news of good food to be had in Mendocino—especially the good breakfasts—spread. Today food critics praise her restaurant. One wrote that it was "the best place to eat breakfast in California." Another claimed that the brunches at Café Beaujolais were "so good that they'll change your whole concept of the meal."

"Customers," Margaret believes, "have never seen a correct rendition of something they thought they knew so well that they don't even think about it anymore. For me, that's what my restaurant is all about . . . making people re-evaluate what they thought was obvious." Now thirty-three, Margaret possesses impressive credentials. The woman who, as a girl mulled over Julia Child's cookbooks, now sits on panels with her. She has her own bakery, her own line of baked goods, and her own cookbook. "Now I'm the boss," she says, "and even though I'm a slave to my business, it's the business that I love."

 RICOTTA PANCAKES

This is a light, creamy pancake, with a flavor so complete that even my beloved maple syrup is superfluous.

4 eggs, separated
1 cup ricotta cheese
⅓ cup small curd cottage cheese
⅔ cup flour
1 pinch salt (about ⅛ teaspoon)
1½ teaspoons baking powder
¾ cup milk

Using an electric mixer, thoroughly blend all the ingredients, except for the egg whites. Beat them until stiff, but not dry, and fold into the mixture.

Heat the griddle, but make sure it is not too hot lest the pancakes scorch. Pour enough batter onto the greased griddle to form 3-inch pancakes. Let them cook until bubbles pop on the top—about 1½ minutes. Peek under one pancake to check the color; when it is a rich brown color, flip it. Cook for about 1¼ minutes more. Do not press down on the pancakes with a spatula to speed up the cooking time.

This batter is best when made just before it is used. The recipe makes about 16 pancakes, each 3 inches in diameter.

FRESH SALMON CHOWDER

Just the dish to show off very fresh salmon. The color is as beautiful as the flavor.

STOCK
The carcass, including head and tail, of one salmon
12 cups water
2 stalks celery, coarsely chopped
2 peeled carrots, coarsely chopped
2 onions, coarsely chopped
1 bay leaf

CHOWDER
1 pound salmon fillet, scaled but not skinned
1 onion, finely chopped
¼ cup unsalted butter
½ teaspoon fresh oregano, finely chopped
½ teaspoon fresh basil, finely chopped
3 pinches saffron
3 cloves garlic, minced
1 cup carrots, minced
¾ cup very thinly sliced celery
⅔ cup uncooked long-grain white rice
1 cup dry white wine
Salt and pepper

GARNISH
8 thin lemon slices, seeded
½ cup sour cream or whipped crème fraîche
2 tablespoons parsley, finely minced

Place all the ingredients for the stock in a pot and simmer for 40 minutes. Occasionally skim the gray foam from the top and discard it. Strain the stock through a fine sieve, discard the bones and vegetables, and reserve the stock.

Return the stock to a clean pot and bring to a simmer. Immerse the scaled salmon fillet or fillets into the stock. The thickest part of the fillet determines the cooking time, which should be 5 minutes of poaching for each 1 inch of thickness. Do *not* under any circumstances overcook the fish. When it is done, remove the salmon from the stock with a slotted spoon, skin, and cool. Separate the fillets into small chunks, not into little pieces like canned tuna.

In a 4-quart saucepan, sauté the onions in butter until they are translucent, about 5 minutes. Add the oregano, basil, saffron, garlic, carrots, celery, and rice. Pour in the white wine and the salmon stock. Simmer for about 15 minutes, until the rice is cooked. Adjust the seasoning. Add the salmon chunks and simmer for another 3 minutes.

Serve immediately in heated bowls, each garnished with a slice of lemon, a dollop of sour cream or whipped *crème fraîche*, and a sprinkling of parsley.

FRIED POLENTA

A very flexible dish.

*1 pound sausage meat, sautéed and drained (Margaret's local
    butcher makes a particularly delicious blend and she
    advises cooks to search out a high-quality sausage for
    themselves.)*
5 cups water
1 teaspoon salt
1²⁄₃ cups polenta *(coarse-grained cornmeal)*
2 tablespoons butter
¹⁄₃ cup toasted pine nuts
¹⁄₂ cup cornmeal
¹⁄₂ cup unsalted butter

Boil the water with the salt and slowly add the *polenta*, stirring constantly.
Reduce the heat and continue stirring for 15 minutes. Add the 2 tablespoons butter, the pine nuts, and sausage and stir to combine. Pour into a
buttered 8 by 4 by 3-inch loaf pan. Cover with plastic wrap and refrigerate
overnight, or for at least 8 hours.

   To unmold, dip the loaf pan into a larger pan of hot water for a few seconds. Use a knife to loosen the sides gently, and invert onto a flat surface;
remove the pan. Slice into pieces ³⁄₄-inch thick and dredge in the dry cornmeal. Melt the ¹⁄₂ cup butter in a pan and, when it's hot, add the *polenta*
slices. Cook over a medium heat until golden brown, about 10 minutes. Flip
the slices and fry the other side.

   Serve with maple syrup for breakfast, accompanied by eggs and biscuits.
Or, for a lunch or dinner entrée, add tomato sauce and grated cheese and
place in a 350°F oven for five minutes.

This bread makes a delicious sandwich with the simplest fillings, such as ripe to-matoes, crunchy lettuce, and a dab of homemade mayonnaise, or very rare roast beef and a strong mustard.

6 tablespoons unsalted butter
6 tablespoons minced garlic
2 packages (¼ ounces each) dry yeast
½ cup minced green onions
4 teaspoons sugar
¼ cup warm water
2 eggs, beaten
1 teaspoon salt
1½ cups dry white wine
6 to 6½ cups all-purpose flour
1 pound aged Asiago or dry Monterey Jack cheese, cut into
  ½-inch cubes

Sauté the onions and garlic in butter for about 30 seconds without letting them brown.

Dissolve the yeast and sugar in water. Stir and set in a warm place for 5 minutes; the mixture should be bubbly. Stir again.

In a large bowl, whisk together the yeast mixture with the eggs, salt, and wine. Gradually, add 3 cups of the flour and, with a large whisk, beat for about 3 minutes until elastic threads start to form around the edge of the bowl. Add the cooled onion and garlic mixture and, with a sturdy wooden spoon, beat in 2½ to 3 more cups of flour. Try to incorporate as much as you can with the spoon.

Turn the dough out onto a very lightly floured board and knead until it is smooth and springy. It tends to be slightly tacky, which is fine. Cover with a clean dry dish towel and let rest for 5 minutes.

Knead again. The dough should not be tacky at this point. If it is, add flour, a tablespoon at a time, kneading after each addition. Do not go overboard and dump on too much flour—one of the most frequently made mistakes in bread making. Remember, you always have to knead for an extra 5 minutes after the last addition of flour.

Place the dough in a large, greased bowl. Turn the ball of dough so that it is greased all over and seal the bowl airtight with plastic wrap. Put in a warm place and let it rise until doubled, about 1 hour. Punch down, turn out, and knead a few times to pop the air bubbles.

Divide the dough in half and knead half of the cheese into each piece. Form the dough into 2 balls. If you wish to bake these as they are, place the balls on a lightly greased baking sheet and press each to flatten it slightly. Otherwise, grease two 9 by 5-inch loaf pans and shape each ball into a log long enough so that the dough touches the ends of the pan. Cover lightly with a dry dish towel and let the dough rise until almost doubled, about 1 hour.

Preheat the oven to 375°F and bake for 25 minutes. Reverse the pans (top to bottom, back to front) and bake for another 5 to 15 minutes. Loaves in pans will take longer than the free-form ones. Check for doneness by tapping the bread on the bottom; the loaves will sound hollow when done. Remove the loaves from the pans and let them cool on wire racks for at least 30 minutes before slicing.

CHOCOLATE
BREAD & BUTTER PUDDING

SERVES SIX

Decadent and homey at the same time, this comfort food par excellence practically defies you to stop eating it. Enjoy this with friends who are not appalled by overindulgence.

½ cup real chocolate chips
Bread, cake or brioche, *sufficient to line the bottom of an 8*
   by 8-inch pan
2 tablespoons unsalted butter
3 eggs
2 egg yolks
½ cup brown sugar
Pinch salt
1¼ cups milk
1½ cups heavy cream
1½ teaspoons pure vanilla extract
⅛ teaspoon nutmeg
⅛ teaspoon cinnamon
Whipped cream

Sprinkle the chocolate chips on the bottom of an unbuttered 8 by 8-inch pan. Slice the bread very thinly; no more than ¼ inch thick. Butter the bread, cake, or *brioche*, and place the slices on the layer of chips. Do *not* crowd the slices; you should be able to see between the layers.

Mix together the eggs, egg yolks, sugar, salt, milk, heavy cream, vanilla, nutmeg, and cinnamon. Pour the mixture through a strainer into the pan.

Push the floating slices down into the egg mixture, although they won't stay. Set the pan into a second pan, measuring about 9 by 13 by 2 inches;

44 · MARGARET FOX

and partially filled with hot water. To minimize the likelihood of spilling water all over the floor, fill the larger pan with water after you have placed it in the oven.

Bake at 325°F for 55 minutes. Do not let the temperature go above 325°F or the custard will separate.

Cool the pudding for at least 1 hour. Serve with whipped cream.

Elka Gilmore

ELKA GILMORE
CAMELIONS · SANTA MONICA

ELKA GILMORE really is a prodigy. At the age of twelve, she entered the restaurant business as a dishwasher—she had decided to write a book on dishwashing—at Café Camille in Austin, Texas. When the pastry chef there left to open his own place, the Swedish Hill Bakery, Elka followed him. She learned to make croissants and pastries in the mornings before high school. By the time she was sixteen, she had dropped out of school (the University of Wisconsin) to become chef of L'Étoile, the leading French restaurant in Madison. "I guess I was precocious!" she remarked.

Deciding she needed more experience, she went to New York City, but "hated it there." So she moved to Boston, where she worked for two and a half years, first at Rebecca's and then at Romagnoli's Table. She started as *sous chef* at Rebecca's, then became chef. While there she took classes with Madeleine Kamman. In 1980 she met her current partner, Marsha Sands, who was then running The Summer House Restaurant in Nantucket and who was "desperate" for a chef at the time. "She would have hired anyone who showed up. She was lucky it was me!"

Marsha, a native of Los Angeles, decided she wanted to open a restaurant there. Elka elected to go first to France, to study and acquire more experience. A friend of Marsha's, whom Elka had met in Los Angeles, owned the Loucallan Hotel in a small town in Provence. Elka went to work with the male chef there and became the American chef *en visite*, which meant that she created a couple of items for the daily menu. In retrospect, she finds her French experience valuable: "It was an opportunity to see the quality

47

of ingredients. It's real obvious why the French sauces are the way they are. The butter here just isn't so wonderful. You don't want to do a sauce that's primarily emulsified butter here. I guess that's why I got so fat in France." But Elka was lonely in Provence. She spoke little French. Being the only woman in a traditional French kitchen was incredibly isolating. "I'm not a loner type of person. I really thrive on community. Besides, it's hard enough to keep up your self image [even] when people are telling you you're great. And it takes a while to get it back. I felt guilty for feeling bad, like I wasn't tough enough, not strong enough to cope." Intending to stay a year, Elka returned to Los Angeles after only six months.

She immediately began looking for a restaurant. One day she saw a "for rent" sign on a prime Santa Monica property. The courtyard building had once been the studio of an architect, John Byers. A historical landmark, it couldn't be structurally changed. Negotiations were long and difficult, but the restaurant opened in December, 1983.

The first name the two women considered, "Bougainvillea," was rejected as being too hard to spell. Marsha suggested the more romantic "Magnolia." Elka thought of "Camellia" and someone punned "Chameleon." In a dictionary, Elka found the Middle English spelling, "camelion," which was defined as "constantly changing." The word was appropriate: they had envisaged a restaurant at which the menu changed every day—even though those changes require apparently endless hours of labor.

During the interview, Elka goes to work to replace a lunch cook mysteriously absent from a shift. She talks to the woman who delivers her herbs (they're grown in a back yard in the San Fernando Valley), to a supplier of vinegars, and to me, as she chops red and yellow peppers, shapes crab cakes, and strains a vegetable purée.

Asked to describe her food, she hesitates. "Regional? The terms 'California cuisine' or 'California-French cuisine' are meaningless. There are no catchwords to describe what I do. I simply start with the highest possible quality of ingredients, generally from the immediate area, and then create dishes based on my range of experience and exposure. I've worked with traditional French and Italian techniques, so what I do is fairly eclectic. Like the *carpaccio* of raw tuna, a kind of Italian *sushi*. Now that chefs are such a big deal, it's easier to be really personal. At least the great chefs—like Wolfgang Puck—take their own intimate experience and make personal statements. 'California cuisine,' " she joked, "That's $30 or more a person and the grill!"

Elka Gilmore recently won the California Seafood Cup, in an invitational competition for which ten chefs from all over the state—"top of the line folks"—entered original recipes for a blind judging. Elka's creation, a plate of two mousses made up of two fish each, three sauces, stuffed baby Japanese eggplants, and fried risotto cakes, won her the chance to compete in the American Seafood Challenge, a national event sponsored by the American Culinary Federation, the group that determines the qualifications of the American Culinary Olympic Team. Participation in this kind of an organization is something new for Elka. Most members are very traditional old-school chefs. "I'm the first to admit I'm media hungry. I'm in this to promote and to support my career. The worst that could happen is that I don't like it. You know, I'm the type who goes on a roller coaster not because I want to, but because I don't want to be forty without having done it. I have to push myself to take risks."

Asked if her joining such a traditional organization represents compromise, she answers, "I've yet to discover the answer to not having to prostitute oneself to a certain extent and still support oneself. If I did exactly what I wanted to—produce the absolute best cuisine—I'd have a restaurant that no one knew about with fifteen tables and only open at dinner."

Not all organizations are alien. Elka is the organizing force behind the Los Angeles–based Women's Culinary Alliance, which she helped found late in 1986, feeling that there was a need for an organization that would provide a sense of community for women in the food business. She must have been at the right place at the right time. The WCA has grown from a small core group to a paid membership of more than 150 in less than six months. Monthly meetings feature seminars ranging from discussions of the effects of new immigration legislation on kitchen staffs to demonstrations of pastry making. Elka knows that she is working in a very competitive industry. With the other board members of the WCA, Susan Fine and Mary Sweeney, she has shaped an organization with an atmosphere to counteract the competition, an atmosphere conducive to good communication. The large number and wide range of members—chefs, executive chefs, caterers, writers, public relations professionals, wine merchants, muffin distributors—is testimony to the timeliness of her social vision, just as the tremendous critical and financial success of Camelions is evidence of her creative vision.

SOFT-SHELLED CRAB SALAD

The warmth and crunchiness of the crabs is set off by the coolness of the lettuce. It's a nice summer dish.

CHERVIL-TRUFFLE MAYONNAISE
1 egg yolk
1 tablespoon lemon juice
¼ cup olive oil
¼ cup peanut oil
1 teaspoon chopped black truffle
2 tablespoons fresh chervil, minced
2 tablespoons heavy cream
Salt, white pepper, and cayenne pepper

SALAD
4 bunches baby oak leaf lettuce or 2 heads limestone lettuce
4 ears corn, kernels cut off and blanched for less than 1 minute
1 tablespoon black truffles, cut into a thin julienne (optional) or 6 shiitake mushrooms, sliced and sautéed
16 baby carrots, cut diagonally into thin slices and blanched
8 soft-shelled crabs, cleaned
About 1 cup each yellow cornmeal and pastry flour, mixed
Curry powder, cayenne pepper, salt, and white pepper
Butter for sautéeing

Whisk the egg yolk with the lemon juice and then slowly whisk in the oils. Add the truffle, chervil, and cream and season to taste with the salt, pepper, and cayenne.

Arrange the lettuce, corn, truffles or mushrooms, and carrots on salad plates.

Dredge the crabs in the cornmeal and pastry flour mixture that has been seasoned with curry powder, cayenne pepper, salt, and white pepper. Sauté the crabs in whole (i.e., not clarified) butter for 2 minutes on each side. Cut each in half and arrange on the salad plates.

Drizzle with the chervil-truffle mayonnaise and garnish with truffles, capers, and chervil sprigs.

*The angel hair pasta is the reason that Camelions exists today. We sell at least
500 portions a week.*

8 ounces cappellini
2 tablespoons basil, cut into a chiffonnade
*2 tablespoons Italian parsley, leaves removed and finely
   chopped*
2 cloves garlic, finely chopped
1 tablespoon unsalted butter
1 tablespoon olive oil
4 sun-dried, oil-cured tomatoes, finely chopped
Salt and black pepper
1 red bell pepper, roasted, peeled, and cut en julienne
1 green bell pepper, roasted, peeled, and cut en julienne
2 tablespoons Parmesan cheese, finely grated

Cook pasta in boiling, salted water.

Mix all other ingredients in a sauté pan and heat through. Mix with pasta
and top with grated Parmesan cheese.

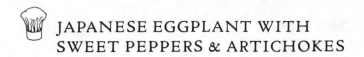

JAPANESE EGGPLANT WITH SWEET PEPPERS & ARTICHOKES

This is probably the second most popular dish at the restaurant. It's the cold version of the angel hair pasta, with the addition of the eggplant.

8 Japanese eggplants, cut into halves
¼ cup regular olive oil
1 bunch fresh basil
2 cloves garlic
Kosher salt and black pepper
1 yellow pepper
1 red pepper
1 green pepper
2 artichokes
Half a lemon

VINAIGRETTE
¼ cup virgin olive oil
2 tablespoons balsamic vinegar

Marinate the halved eggplants, for at least 30 minutes, in a mixture of the regular olive oil, 1 tablespoon of basil, cut *en chiffonnade*, and 1 clove of the garlic, finely chopped. Salt and pepper them and then grill them on both sides.

Roast and peel the peppers and cut each into 4 equal pieces. Trim the artichokes and boil them, until tender, with the half lemon. Remove the artichoke leaves and the choke and cut each artichoke bottom into four slices.

Make a vinaigrette with the rest of the basil, the second clove of garlic, the virgin olive oil, and the balsamic vinegar.

Assemble the salad and serve it cold or at room temperature.

GRILLED SWORDFISH WITH BLOOD ORANGE SALSA

What I like most about this dish is the color of the sauce. The bright orange is set off by the whiteness of the fish. It looks great.

4 swordfish steaks, skinned and cut into steaks weighing 6 or
   7 oz. each
½ cup dry vermouth
½ cup fresh orange juice
2 shallots, cut into thin slices
Salt and white pepper

Marinate the swordfish in a mixture of the vermouth, orange juice, shallots, salt, and white pepper for about 3 hours.

BLOOD ORANGE SALSA
3 blood oranges (navel oranges may be substituted), sectioned
1 onion, thinly sliced and sautéed
Enough orange juice to moisten
1 tablespoon peanut oil
1 tablespoon cilantro, finely chopped

Combine all the ingredients, adding the cilantro to taste, and let *salsa* marinate for about an hour.

Cook the swordfish on a grill or under a broiler for about 2 or 3 minutes on each side. Garnish with *salsa*.

# RABBIT & FIG RAGOUT

The idea is to have a sweet sauce with a very foreign flavor. Nobody was interested in this dish until it was in Gourmet; *then everyone wanted it.*

1 rabbit weighing about 3 pounds, boned completely,
  trimmed, and cut into 1-inch cubes
2 tablespoons sweet butter
Salt to taste
12 fresh black Mission figs, cut into halves
1 bunch leeks, cut into a fine julienne

SAUCE
1 quart rabbit, or chicken, stock
3 tablespoons red wine vinegar
1 cup ruby-type port
2 shallots
2 sprigs fresh thyme
2 bay leaves
12 fresh black Mission figs, chopped
4 ounces sweet butter
Salt to taste

Make the sauce first. Flavor the rabbit, or chicken, stock with the vinegar, port, and shallots and reduce the mixture by half. Add the herbs and figs and reduce by half again. Purée and strain. Finish with the sweet butter and salt to taste.

Sauté the rabbit in the butter over medium heat until it is half cooked, about 3 minutes. Sprinkle the meat with salt while it is cooking. Add the leeks and cook until they are soft. Add the figs and the sauce and cook for another 3 minutes. Garnish with chopped Italian parsley.

Joyce Goldstein

JOYCE GOLDSTEIN

SQUARE ONE · CAFFÈ QUADRO
SAN FRANCISCO

IN THIS CITY of talented chefs," begins *Bon Appétit*, "there is no brighter star than Joyce Goldstein, kitchen designer, writer, former chef at Chez Panisse Café in Berkeley and creator of San Francisco's first international cooking school." Her restaurant, Square One (and the smaller Caffè Quadro next door) is regarded by critics as being one of the best in the state.

In 1980 Joyce started at Chez Panisse Café, purely by chance. Her son, a busboy there, told her they needed some extra help. "I was scared to death when I got there," she says. "Chez Panisse is a place where they never explain things to you, which means I was paranoid for a long time." She started by making breads, pizza, and pasta, and later moved on to "prepping" and making soups and salads. "Eventually, I ended up doing all the recipes, doing all the marketing, doing all the staff training and management of the Café—a ridiculous job! But I loved it . . . I love to work!" She stayed at Chez Panisse Café for three years.

At some point, it occurred to her that, instead of working to serve more than 550 customers a day there, she could open her own restaurant. Square One was born. "We were all sitting around in a meeting," Joyce explains, "when someone said, 'That's it. Everyday it's like starting over again . . . back to square one.'" The name stuck.

Joyce is a realist with plenty of advice to give the would-be restaurateur or chef. At Square One, after hearing that an employee was sick and unable to come in for that evening's "prep," she turned and said, "That's it in a nutshell. You're open whether someone's sick or not. There are so many positions that need to be filled; you have to do it." She believes that the novice should work in a restaurant first, before going to cooking school, "to learn about the hard work and long hours that are not part of the glamorous aura. Study the classics before trying to improvise your own dishes," she advises.

She doesn't consider herself as a producer of California cuisine, nor does she believe that her food is really experimental. Instead, she compares her cooking to traveling, which she has done extensively. "I want to take foods from specific cultures and do the best version of a particular dish that I can possibly do." In her unconventional cookbook, *Feedback*, she writes, "By being independent and personal, you won't have to pay attention to fads and fashion in foods and menu planning. I read recently in a magazine that *moussaka* was 'out' this year and *gazpacho* was 'in'. Really, who cares? Who calls the shots, your mouth or your social insecurity?"

Consequently, a very personal and international approach characterizes Square One's menu, yet one country stands out—Italy; Italy and pasta. While living in Rome in 1959 Joyce, having decided to find the city's best *spaghetti carbonara*, sampled the dish at fifty-two restaurants. Net gain—a winner, a palate refined, and twenty extra pounds. She took the weight off, but kept her title of "pasta maniac." Talking about pasta with Joyce is almost as much fun as eating it. "There's a lot of faddishness involved. Pasta has been so misunderstood and so mistreated," simply for the sake of innovation, she says. For instance, Joyce refuses to cook *pasta primavera*, in California a popular dish in which assorted vegetables are combined with *spaghetti* or *fettuccine*. "You might as well be eating stir-fried Chinese vegetables," she complains. Even those who like *pasta primavera* might, on listening to her talk about pasta as being "more than the sum of its parts" change their minds. "Pasta must have a unifying element. The Italians have been doing pasta for a very long time, understanding that certain sauces work well with dried pasta, certain sauces work well with fresh pasta, that there are certain magic combinations."

Certainly Square One is full of those magic combinations . . . not only from Italy, but also from the Middle East, India, France, and San Francisco.

 ROASTED EGGPLANT SOUP SERVES FOUR

2 small to medium eggplants
1 large eggplant
3 tablespoons sweet butter
1 yellow onion, sliced
4 cups chicken stock (and a bit more to thin the soup)
½ cup heavy cream (optional)
Salt and pepper

Preheat the oven to 450°F. Prick the two small or medium eggplants with a fork. Bake for about an hour, until the eggplants are very tender. Turn once so that they cook evenly. Remove from the oven when done, and drain in a colander until cool.

Preheat the broiler to low. Broil the large eggplant, turning it occasionally, until the skin is charred on all sides and the flesh tender inside. This may take about 20 minutes. You may also grill the eggplant on a heavy griddle on top of the stove, with a medium flame under the griddle. This may take a little less time, but you need to have a very heavy griddle so that the eggplant cooks evenly and won't scorch and turn bitter. Place the grilled eggplant on a drainer tray or in a colander. Cool. When the eggplants are cool enough to handle, cut them in half and scoop out the flesh.

Melt the butter in a saucepan. Add the onions and sauté over medium heat, stirring occasionally, until the onions are tender and translucent. Add the chicken stock and eggplant pulp and bring to a boil. Simmer for a few minutes, then purée the soup in a blender or food processor.

Thin the soup to the desired consistency. If the eggplant flavor is too smoky for your palate, add the cream. Season to taste with salt and pepper. Appropriate garnishes for this soup are: whipped cream flavored with lemon zest; chopped tomatoes and a basil chiffonnade; whipped cream flavored with pesto; or a purée of roasted peppers.

ALASKAN HALIBUT CURED WITH GIN & JUNIPER

2 pounds fillet of halibut, in 1 piece and with skin on 1 side
2 tablespoons kosher salt
4 tablespoons sugar
$\frac{1}{4}$ teaspoon freshly ground black pepper
$\frac{1}{4}$ teaspoon ground allspice
2 tablespoons juniper berries, ground coarsely in a spice mill
The peel from 1 large or 2 medium oranges, cut into strips
    about 3 inches long and $\frac{1}{4}$ inch wide, with the white pith
    removed
2 tablespoons Bombay gin

Place fish fillet, skin-side down, in noncorrosive pan or dish.

Combine the salt, sugar, pepper, allspice, and juniper berries and rub this mixture onto the fish. Place the strips of orange peel atop the fish. Sprinkle with gin. Cover the fish with plastic wrap. Place another pan atop the fish and weight it down, not too heavily. Refrigerate.

Baste the fish daily, for 3 days, with the liquid that accumulates around it. Remove the weights after 2 days.

Serve, thinly sliced, accompanied by thinly sliced cucumbers and *daikon* (dressed with white vinegar, sugar, water, and a bit of salt), and *wasabi* cream.

WASABI CREAM

2 tablespoons wasabi
2 tablespoons white vinegar
½ cup sour cream
½ cup barely whipped heavy cream
1 to 2 teaspoons sugar, to taste

Mix the *wasabi* powder with the vinegar and let the mixture sit for 5 minutes. Then fold in the sour cream and the heavy cream and add the sugar to taste. Then add a bit more vinegar or perhaps sugar until you have the proper balance.

GRILLED SPICED SQUAB IN AN ALGERIAN MARINADE

6 squab, weighing about 1 pound each
1 small bunch cilantro, chopped, to yield 4 tablespoons
4 green onions, chopped, to yield 4 tablespoons
4 cloves of garlic, peeled
2-inch piece of fresh ginger, peeled and sliced
2 tablespoons aniseed, pan toasted and crushed
½ teaspoon saffron filaments, chopped fine
1 tablespoon paprika
1 teaspoon cayenne
½ cup lemon juice
1½ cups light olive oil
Freshly ground black pepper, to taste
Salt to taste, just before cooking

Remove the head and feet from the squab. Insert a sharp knife through the neck cavity and carefully split the bird down the back, keeping the breast intact. Remove the backbone, then carefully remove the breast bone, central cartilage, and ribs. The bird should look like a butterfly, with only wing and leg bones attached.

Chop the cilantro and green onions and set aside. In a food processor blend the garlic cloves and fresh ginger slices to a paste. Add the spices and lemon juice, and pulse to combine, for about 30 seconds. Put the blended ingredients into a bowl, add the chopped cilantro and green onions, and blend in the olive oil with a whisk. Add freshly ground black pepper to taste. The marinade should be a little spicy!

Place the squab in a shallow, noncorrosive container and pour over the marinade. Cover and place in the refrigerator overnight. Bring the squab to room temperature before grilling.

Preheat broiler or an outdoor grill to highest temperature. Sprinkle squab with salt. Grill squab, skin-side up, for 4 minutes, then turn to grill for 3 minutes on the skin side. Squab are best served rare; the longer you cook them, the tougher they become. The home gas or electric broiler will take longer than mesquite or charcoal briquettes. Fires vary considerably in intensity. Test squab for doneness rather than trusting to the times suggested here, which are for a very hot fire.

Serve the squab with *couscous*, rice, or a combination of *bulghur* wheat and rice, sprinkled with minced green onions and accompanied by lemon wedges.

TANDOORI-STYLE ROAST CHICKEN

1 onion, cut in chunks
2 cloves of garlic, chopped
¼ cup lime (or lemon) juice
1 tablespoon ground coriander
½ teaspoon cayenne pepper
2 teaspoons paprika
1 teaspoon ground ginger
¼ teaspoon ground cloves
¼ teaspoon ground cardamom
½ teaspoon turmeric
½ teaspoon salt
Freshly ground black pepper, to taste
2 cups unflavored yoghurt
6 poussin *or baby chickens, each weighing about 1 pound*

Place the onion and garlic in the container of a food processor. Purée and add the lime juice. Then add the spices and yoghurt and process well.

Marinate the six little chickens in the yoghurt mixture overnight, in the refrigerator.

Preheat the oven to 450°F. Bring the chickens to room temperature. Remove some of the marinade from the birds. Roast them for about 40 to 45 minutes. Sprinkle with additional paprika. Serve with saffron rice, a chutney of your choice, and curried spinach or broccoli.

You may use this marinade on chicken halves, and broil or grill them. Or you may use the marinade on pieces of chicken, to be broiled or baked. The individual bird makes a pretty presentation, but you could skewer pieces of marinated chicken, broil, and serve as a *tandoori brochette*. The *brochette* pieces may be skinless and boneless. They will marinate more quickly, in 4 to 8 hours.

 HONEY MOUSSE

6 egg yolks
¾ cup honey
1 cup heavy cream, or a bit more
Shaved chocolate

Beat the egg yolks with honey until they are very pale and thick. Whip the cream until it's stiff and fold into the honey mixture. Ladle into individual serving dishes or a bowl. Top with shaved chocolate. Cover with a double thickness of tinfoil, and place in the freezer for at least 4 hours.

Before serving, remove from freezer and place in refrigerator for 1 hour for small molds; a few hours for a large bowl. This mousse will keep frozen for 2 months.

Mimi Hébert

MIMI HÉBERT

CHEZ HÉLÈNE · BEVERLY HILLS

MIMI HÉBERT runs a French-Canadian *auberge* in the middle of Beverly Hills. After twelve years in funky Venice, Chez Hélène has moved uptown. "Our lease ran out and I decided it was time for a change," says Mimi. With characteristic style, she hasn't changed her prices. In the only house among elegant boutiques and expensive hotels, the new Chez Hélène looks—as did the old—like a home you would like to live in, with its dark wood antiques, fireplace, and chandeliers made for candles instead of electricity. The design she wanted has not been easy to keep. "Last week they made me cry," says Mimi, looking up at two intruding spotlights, which were ordered by the fire department. "My beautiful ceiling! It's so frustrating to achieve a certain *décor* and have it destroyed by what the city obliges you to have."

In moving, Mimi had to start over again. "I realized that in Venice nothing was up to the code. We didn't have any exit signs, nor any official capacity rating. The rules have changed a lot in twelve years. Now it's difficult to open your own place." She has been unable to use the new building's open attic, where the exposed beams would have been perfect for drying strings of herbs—as they are dried in Canadian country houses. After she had already begun to design the restaurant around that space, she heard from the city that she could use it only if all the wood were fireproofed— at a cost of $20,000. "Before you start," she says, "make sure you find out exactly what the rules are."

Mimi grew up in Quebec and went to a Roman Catholic school run by nuns. There she learned to bake her first cake, to concoct her first soup. Her early years at home also nurtured a love for cooking. Her family's roots extend to Normandy and Brittany, regions famous for excellent provincial cuisine, for heavy cream and butter, seafood, and Calvados. Later she studied French cuisine with Professor Henri Bernard in Montreal. Gault and Millau liked her style enough to award Chez Hélène a toque in their latest guide to the restaurants of Los Angeles.

"French-Canadian cuisine is heavy food, very tasty and it's not fancy," she says. "To the contrary, nothing is flambéed. It's really peasant food. I use a lot of mustard and *herbes de Provence*." Mimi believes that this style of cooking has all but disappeared from Quebec, only revived for the holidays.

When she first started at Chez Hélène, she was everything—chef, waitress, and dishwasher. She was soon invited to become a partner, but that didn't decrease her work load. Eventually, Mimi became the sole owner. In retrospect, she says: "My first sign that I would make it was when I saw customers coming back. For me, this is the best sign. If you have customers coming once, that's easy. You just have to have reviews and publicity. But to keep them coming back—that's the hard part." Many of Mimi's old customers have followed her from Venice to Beverly Hills.

Chez Hélène is probably the only French-Canadian restaurant in the state, a fact she is proud of. "There's a tendency now to open restaurants that are all the same," she says. "I do the kind of cooking I like to do. I can cook *nouvelle*, but what I prefer most is simple, peasant cuisine." One critic called her food "honest," a word that certainly describes her *tourtière* or *chômeur*. Mimi advises would-be restaurateurs to "be sure you love it before you go into it," but at the same time feels that there really is no other business for herself. "I feel very lucky . . . I love my work. Every morning I get up and I'm happy to go to work. For me it's the only way."

 CRETONS À L'ANCIENNE

POTTED PORK

I give a little bit of this to everyone who comes into my restaurant. I really like the idea that when people sit down with their bread they will have a little something to go with it. But just a little bit . . . I want them to have room for everything else.

1 pound ground pork
1 cup bread crumbs
1 onion, grated or minced
Pinches of salt, pepper, ground cloves, and ground cinnamon
1 cup milk

Put all of the ingredients into a pot. Cover and cook over low heat for 1 hour, stirring occasionally.

Pour into a bowl and allow to cool. Serve on toast.

SAUCISSES À LA BIÈRE

SAUSAGES WITH BEER

This is a popular dish for us. What impresses me about it is that I always thought the dish was for hardworking men—it is very hearty food—but it is a luncheon favorite among the most delicate women. The beer gives the sausages a sweet taste; you can't actually detect a beer flavor.

4 ounces butter
2 pounds mild Italian sausages (approximately 6 sausages)
2 onions, sliced
1½ to 2¼ cups (1 to 1½ bottles or cans, 12 ounces each)
   beer—dark beer will give a slightly bitter flavor
2 cans (16 ounces each) peeled tomatoes
4 tablespoons fresh basil
Salt and pepper

Melt the butter in a heavy saucepan, being careful not to let it burn. Sauté the sausages until they are browned. Add the onions, and sauté them until they are transparent.

Add the beer, tomatoes, basil, salt, and pepper. Cover and simmer for 30 minutes or more.

Serve over rice.

I always like to use fresh ingredients, but this soufflé comes out better with canned corn. When fresh corn is used the texture suffers.

3 eggs
2 tablespoons sugar
Pinch of salt
1 can (16 ounces) cream-style corn
2 ounces butter, melted
½ cup milk
3½ tablespoons flour
2 teaspoons baking powder

In a bowl, beat the eggs well and then add the rest of the ingredients in the order in which they are given above. Pour this mixture into 8 buttered ramekins. Bake at 425°F for 15 to 20 minutes, until puffed up and golden.

RAGOÛT DES PATTES DE COCHON

BRAISED PIGS' TROTTERS

The skin is what really gives a lot of flavor to this dish, so don't remove it until you are ready to serve. Let me suggest that you serve the ragout with beets and mashed potatoes.

2 to 3 pounds of pigs' feet, cut into slices
1 teaspoon salt
¼ teaspoon pepper
½ teaspoon ground cinnamon
¼ teaspoon ground cloves
⅛ teaspoon ground nutmeg
2 tablespoons fat
4 to 6 cups warm water
1 cup roasted onion
4 tablespoons flour
½ cup water

Rub the pigs' feet in a mixture of salt, pepper, cinnamon, cloves, and nutmeg. Melt the fat in a heavy skillet. Cook the pork until brown. When it's ready, add the warm water and roasted onion. Cover and cook slowly until the meat is tender, about 2 hours. Remove the skin.

Grill or brown the flour by heating a cast-iron pan until it is medium hot, sprinkling the flour over the hot surface, and shaking the pan or stirring the flour as it colors. This is a quick process, but be careful not to burn the flour.

Mix the browned flour and the water. Pour it over the stew. Cook until you have a slightly thick sauce.

 CHÔMEUR

CARAMEL
2 cups light brown sugar
¾ cup milk
2 tablespoons butter, chilled and cut into pieces

CAKE
1 egg, beaten
4 tablespoons granulated sugar
½ cup butter, melted
½ cup milk
1 cup flour
1 teaspoon baking powder
1 teaspoon vanilla extract

Preheat oven to 350°F. For the caramel, combine, in a ceramic or glass quart baking dish, the light brown sugar, ¾ cup milk, and pieces of butter.

For the cake, combine the egg, granulated sugar, and melted butter. Add the milk and stir well. Add the flour, baking powder, and vanilla. Spoon onto the caramel.

Bake for 45 to 50 minutes, until golden. Serve with heavy cream.

VARIATION
You can replace the caramel with raspberries.

1 cup fresh raspberries or *1 can (10 ounces) frozen raspberries*
¾ cup granulated sugar
½ cup hot water

Mix the raspberries, sugar, and water together in a quart ceramic or glass baking dish, and then proceed with the cake part of the recipe.

Maggie Blyth Klein

MAGGIE BLYTH KLEIN
OLIVETO · OAKLAND

ASK MAGGIE KLEIN what's in a name. "Naming the place was such a painful process," she says. "I already had my logo, which I got from an Italian newspaper—a peasant in silhouette with laden donkey in an olive grove—but after two years of tossing it around I still didn't have a name." A "naming party" came up with suggestions such as "Chez Vrolet," "Grub Med," and "Maggie's," puns meant to amuse, but doing nothing to get the salivary glands going. Actually, the party did have its effect: the next day one of the original entries was chosen—Oliveto, Italian for "olive grove."

The name is entirely memorable (a good sign) and appropriate. The restaurant offers the northern Mediterranean cuisines of Italy, Spain and France, particularly those of Tuscany and the Basque country. The interior is hung with paintings and photographs of olive groves. And there is space for the big, Tuscan urns for storing olive oil called *orci*. The softly colored, hand-rubbed pastel walls lend a rustic feeling. Interior designers were generous with their advice. They are interested in being creative and trend-setting; Maggie was wanting a European-style, traditional decor. For the windows, "I was thinking stretched linen . . . that looks European; they were thinking stretched burlap that looks modern." Instead of lights projecting upward out of columns, Maggie wanted plain, old light fixtures. An ingenious solution using Italian planters was devised by the builder-designer. Maggie's love of olive lore is presented in her book, *The Feast of the Olive*.

The restaurant is ambitious. Downstairs there is a counter offering everything from Italian egg dishes with *caffè latte* in the morning, Spanish *tapas* with chilled sherry in the late afternoon, to pizza late at night. Upstairs is a formal dining room with its own multicourse menu of *risotto* and *antipasta*, pasta, *osso buco*, and salads of arugula and baby greens dressed with the best Tuscan olive oil. Maggie wanted every aspect of her restaurant to be as authentic as possible. She found out how to compromise. In Spain, those bite-sized treats called *tapas* sit out on the bar counter for all to admire and to choose from: *chorizo*, mussels, eggs, *tortillas*—a cornucopia for everyone. Health regulations in the U.S. prohibit such earthy presentations, so her plates of squid in its own ink have to be refrigerated.

Maggie is a self-taught cook, who for years worked as a journalist and editor. One skill from her previous career has served her well in opening Oliveto—research. She had never really worked full-time in a restaurant before working in her own, but she has researched many. Journalism gave her a view into different restaurant environments. She spent a day with a Korean couple to see how a mom-and-pop shop makes it; it was a sixteen-hour day of hard work. She began at four o'clock one morning at Fournou's Ovens in San Francisco to explore the hotel restaurant world. The real adventures started when she became an employee of several restaurants so as to learn how Oliveto should work. In one she learned how a complex restaurant computer system operated; in another, she did all the monotonous chores—washing dishes, chopping vegetables, making mayonnaise. "I wanted to get an idea of what each job entailed," she says. The worst educational experience was working for a large pizza chain. "I would make $24 for three days of the hardest work I have ever done in my life. I even had to buy my own, less than stylish outfit, with a handsome one-third-inch-thick plastic apron." On the night shift she washed dishes, made pizzas and, at one in the morning, mopped the floors before going home. She wanted to find out how they despatched hot to-order pizzas on time.

Maggie has one skill that most journalists lack—the ability to eat something in a restaurant and then replicate it at home. That kind of food sense doesn't come easily. Her abilities as a cook led to much praise from her husband and friends. Eventually their gentle proddings and a desire to work for herself helped her to create Oliveto. "It's the same absurd thing we hear all the time, 'Gee, Mathilde, these muffins are so good you should open a restaurant!' But who would consider that realistic career counseling?" Her advice to would-be restaurateurs is this: "Never forget your vision. Although a restaurant involves countless mundane details, you mustn't forget about what compelled you to open a restaurant in the first place—your passion for a particular kind of food." She adds that it's going to cost an awful lot more than you thought it would, so be prepared. An extra stove downstairs would have cost $10,000, not for the stove itself, but for the ventilation. "I don't think I'm a greedy person," she says. "I just hope I make what I used to as an editor."

TART OF PURÉED CHICKPEAS & ROSEMARY

This rustic appetizer or first course should be served warm from the oven as it is dense and tends to dry as it cools. Served under a layer of fresh-from-the-garden tomato slices, or atop a fresh tomato purée or sauce, it is a fragrant and unusual dish.

CRUST
1¼ cups all-purpose flour
Salt
6 tablespoons butter from the freezer, cut into pieces
2 tablespoons cold vegetable shortening
3 tablespoons iced water

In a mixing bowl, stir the flour and the salt. With a pastry cutter, incorporate into the mixture the butter and shortening until the flour takes on the appearance of coarse meal. Drizzle the iced water over the flour 1 tablespoon at a time, mixing with a fork. Quickly stir to distribute the water until a ball forms, using your fingers only at the very end to keep the temperature down. Dust the ball with flour, wrap it in waxed paper, and refrigerate for at least an hour. Roll the flour out to fit a 9-inch tart or pie pan and complete the shell. Refrigerate until the filling is ready.

FILLING

3 cups cooked chickpeas (garbanzos)
4 eggs
Freshly ground black pepper
1 tablespoon fresh rosemary, minced
Zest of one lemon, grated
1 cup Parmesan cheese, grated
3 large cloves garlic, minced
3 tablespoons olive oil
4 tablespoons sweet butter

Purée the chickpeas using the coarsest fitting of your food mill. In a bowl, mix the chickpeas with the eggs, a good quantity of pepper, rosemary, lemon zest, and Parmesan cheese. In a small pan, sauté the garlic until soft in the olive oil and butter. Incorporate all into the chickpea mixture. Spoon the filling into the prepared crust and smooth with a spatula. Bake in a preheated 350°F oven until the crust is an even golden brown, about 50 minutes. Allow to sit about 5 minutes, then serve warm.

GAMBAS CON HUEVOS Y ESPINACAS

SHRIMP WITH EGGS & SPINACH

SERVES FOUR AS A
FIRST COURSE OR
THREE FOR
LUNCH

It was part of my dream in starting Oliveto to provide authentic Spanish cooking from the countryside of, particularly, Andalucia—a cuisine that is, at best, under-represented in America. Bordered as the country is by two seas, Spain's restaurants and tapa *bars abound with shrimp, served any number of ways. When they are left whole, however, they are never peeled nor are they, of course, deveined. In the following recipe the spices are typically Andalucian; the eggs and peppers are reminiscent of the famous Basque dish,* piparrada.

3 cloves garlic, minced
3 whole cloves
⅛ teaspoon ground cloves
1 bay leaf, broken
1 red bell pepper, very thinly sliced
3 tablespoons olive oil
½ pound (about 20) medium shrimp, unshelled
Hot pepper flakes
1 bunch spinach, chopped coarsely
Salt
4 eggs
¼ teaspoon ground cumin
Lemon slices

In a large skillet or frying pan that has a lid, sauté the garlic, cloves (whole and ground), bay leaf, and pepper slices in some of the olive oil until the pepper is soft. Transfer the pepper slices to a dish and place in a warming oven. Remove the whole cloves and the bay leaf pieces and discard.

In the remaining oil, sauté the shrimp, with hot pepper flakes to taste,

82 · MAGGIE KLEIN

until they are just pink. Add more olive oil if necessary. Transfer the shrimp to a dish and hold in the warming oven.

Without wiping out the pan, add the spinach, sprinkle with salt, cover, and cook until the spinach is just wilted.

Whisk the eggs with the cumin and add to the pan with the red peppers. Use a spatula to stir the eggs as they cook. They are done when they are just set.

Serve in the center of a serving plate surrounded by the shrimp. Have lemon slices available on the table in a separate bowl.

ROAST PORK MARINATED IN SWEET VOUVRAY

For this dish to be successful, the roast must be a tender cut, the wine sweet. Any sweet wine will do—a sweet Chenin Blanc or a Riesling, for example. The plentiful and succulent roasted garlic cloves in the rich sauce are the crowning touch.

A 3-pound pork roast, preferably a boned loin
⅛ teaspoon cardamom
5 whole cloves
¼ stick cinnamon, broken
5 peppercorns
½ bay leaf, crumbled
1 bottle sweet Vouvray or other sweet white wine
Coarse-ground sea salt
Olive oil
1 head garlic
2 tablespoons sweet butter
½ brown (yellow) onion, minced
½ teaspoon granulated sugar
½ cup crème fraîche *or whipping cream*
Salt

Put the roast in a deep, narrow glass or ceramic bowl. Grind the cardamom, cloves, cinnamon, peppercorns, and bay leaf in a mortar or coffee grinder. In a small saucepan, simmer the spices in ½ cup of the wine for 5 minutes, then pour over the pork. Pour the remainder of the wine over the pork, cover with plastic wrap, and refrigerate overnight. (If the meat is not completely submerged, turn it halfway through the marinating time.)

An hour before baking time, remove the pork from the marinade and let it sit at room temperature in its baking pan. Rub with coarse-ground salt and olive oil. Bake in a preheated oven at 375°F for 1 hour and 25 minutes, or until an instant-read thermometer inserted into the fleshiest part of the roast reads 135°.

Meanwhile, as the pork cooks, peel the cloves of one head of garlic. Mince one clove and sauté it in 1 tablespoon of the sweet butter with the onion until lightly browned. Add the marinating liquid and reduce by half. Set aside.

Fabricate a makeshift tray, out of aluminum foil, that will fit into a toaster oven. Put the remaining garlic cloves in the tray with 1 tablespoon sweet butter and put the tray into the toaster oven at 350°F. Roast the garlic cloves for about 5 minutes, then shake to distribute the melted butter and sprinkle with the granulated sugar. Continue to roast the cloves until they are lightly browned and tender, about 15 to 20 minutes more. Remove from the toaster oven and set aside.

Lacking a toaster oven, you can slowly braise the garlic cloves with 1 tablespoon sweet butter, 2 tablespoons stock or water, and the sugar until the garlic is golden and the liquid evaporated.

When the roast is done, transfer it to a carving board to rest. Drain the fat out of the baking pan and discard. Add the reduced marinade to the pan and deglaze over a medium-high heat until there is about 1 cup of liquid. Strain the liquid and wipe the pan clean. Return the strained liquid to the baking pan and, over a low heat, whisk in the *crème fraîche* or cream. Adjust salt, add the garlic cloves, and serve the meat, sliced thin, with the sauce.

FARINA "GNOCCHI" WITH BUTTER & PARMESAN

These "gnocchi" never fail. Because they aren't boiled, there is no chance for them to become tough and rubbery. They are rich but light, making them a satisfying first course or a good accompaniment to any rich stew or osso buco, *topped with* gremolata.

3 cups milk
1 teaspoon salt
¼ teaspoon ground nutmeg
Freshly ground black pepper
¾ cup farina (or Cream of Wheat)
2 eggs, whisked
1½ cups grated Parmesan cheese
4 tablespoons sweet butter, plus enough butter to coat two large pans

To 3 cups milk in a heavy saucepan, add the salt, nutmeg, and a good dash of pepper. Bring the milk to a boil and slowly add the farina, stirring with a wooden spoon as you add. Stir until the mixture is very thick, a few minutes. Remove from the heat and allow to cool slightly.

Combine the eggs with one cup of the cheese and add this mixture to the farina, stirring well to incorporate. Butter a small cookie sheet and, with a spatula, spread the farina mixture onto the sheet until it is a consistent ⅓-inch thick. Refrigerate until firm, about an hour.

Preheat the oven to 425°F. With a cookie cutter or glass measuring about 1½ inches in diameter, cut the farina into rounds, wetting the cutter with water if it sticks. Butter a 9- to 10-inch pie pan or baking dish, and transfer the rounds with a spatula to the pan, overlapping them a bit to form two circles of *gnocchi*. Melt 4 tablespoons of butter and pour it over the *gnocchi*. Top with the remaining ½ cup of cheese, and bake at 425°F for about 20 minutes, or until the *gnocchi* are slightly browned and bubbling. Serve very hot.

MOZZARELLA IN CARROZZA

FRIED MOZZARELLA SANDWICHES

The way you execute this simple recipe for batter-dipped sandwiches will depend on your bread: if the loaf is a large round one, use half slices; if the loaf is narrower (4½ inches by 2½ inches, for example), use the slices whole. Two little sandwiches should fit in the pan at once. If fresh basil is not available, use other fresh herbs, dried tomatoes, or scallions sautéed with minced hot peppers.

4 ounces buffalo or whole milk mozzarella
Fresh basil leaves
8 slices Tuscan-style bread, ½- to ¾-inch thick
6 eggs
1 pint peanut oil
Salt and freshly ground pepper, to taste

Place about 1 ounce cheese per sandwich with a layer of fresh basil leaves between 2 slices of bread. Whisk the eggs together in a mixing bowl. In a heavy 8-inch pan or pot, heat the peanut oil to frying temperature. Test the oil with a cube of bread—if it browns in 1 minute, the oil is at the proper temperature. (If you use a wider pan, you will need more oil. I've found that for this small recipe, even a 2-inch-deep iron pan is adequate.) Dip the sandwiches, 1 at a time, into the eggs and allow the outsides of both sides of the sandwiches to become saturated. Fry the sandwiches 2 at a time, turning them with the tongs as each side becomes golden brown. Transfer to paper toweling, cut the sandwiches in half, salt and pepper them to taste (depending on whether there is salt in the cheese), and serve immediately.

 CITRUS & OLIVE OIL CAKE

While I was researching my cookbook about olives and olive oil, I tasted a zesty and unusual cake made by a friend who is a particularly fine baker. Inspired by the already unique cake, I experimented by substituting olive oil for peanut. The recipe for the result, an even richer cake, with delicate overtones of olive oil, was published in the book. The cake keeps well in the refrigerator for days. It is delicious and moist all by itself, but may be garnished with thin, poached orange slices and a glaze of apricot jam strained over the top, or served with lightly sweetened whipped cream or crème fraîche.

2 small navel oranges
1 lemon
6 ounces almonds
4 eggs
½ teaspoon salt
1½ cups sugar
1 cup all-purpose flour
3 teaspoons baking powder
⅔ cup olive oil

In a small saucepan, cover the oranges and lemon with water and simmer them for half an hour. Drain and let them cool. Cut off the stem ends, and cut the fruit in half; scoop out the pulp and seeds of the lemon and discard. Chop the oranges (with their rind) and lemon rind very fine. Squeeze out as much liquid as you can in a strainer.

Chop the almonds in a blender or food processor until they are almost as fine as crumbs.

Beat the eggs and salt together until very thick and light. Then gradually add the sugar while continuing to beat.

Mix the flour and baking powder and add to the egg mixture until blended. Mix in the fruit, nuts, and olive oil, being careful not to overmix.

Turn the batter into an oiled, 9-inch springform pan. Bake at 350°F for 1 hour, or until a knife inserted into the center comes out clean.

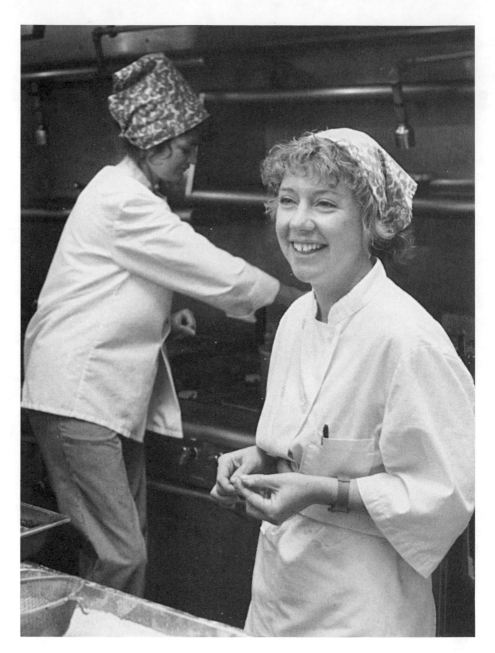

Anne and Wendy Little

WENDY & ANNE LITTLE
THE PLOW & ANGEL · MONTECITO

IT'S RARE to find two sisters working together in the kitchen of an exclusive hotel; rarer still to find one of them as the boss. At the San Ysidro Ranch, near Santa Barbara, Wendy Little is executive chef, her younger sister, Anne, is pastry chef of the restaurant, The Plow and Angel. The Ranch is a private, expensive retreat covering 540 acres of prime canyon land. In 1983, the well-regarded French guide, *Relais et Chateaux*, listed the resort, making it only the second U.S. establishment to be included among the 331 international recommendations. The interior is characterized by thick whitewashed walls, low stone archways, and expansive timber-beam ceilings. The dining room was once a citrus packing house.

According to Wendy, who was talking to a prominent restaurant critic, "There is no magic to my success. I've done well because I'm a hard worker and very reliable. It probably comes from being the oldest of six kids." She began by washing dishes in a vegetarian restaurant, while studying bilingual education at the University of California, Santa Barbara. Instead of graduate work she decided to apprentice with the only French chef in Santa Barbara, Camille Schwartz, who came from Alsace-Lorraine. "He would hire women," she says.

First he showed her the basics—how to bone a fish, turn a carrot, deglaze a pan. Then she went on to learn his buying techniques, his methods of administration, his staff scheduling. She evolved from cook to chef, a very important distinction. After two years Schwartz left and Wendy took his place as executive chef. The opportunity of becoming a chef after such a short time would be inconceivable in Europe. In California, where institutions are less bound by rules and more attuned to nurturing talent, chefs have greater mobility and freedom.

Santa Barbara has become known as a culinary center. The influential Julia Child now divides her time between Cambridge, Massachusetts, and Santa Barbara. Once, while dining at the Ranch, she suggested that Wendy attend La Varenne cooking school in Paris. The school draws most of its students from America; classes are in English and French. The Ranch agreed to pay Wendy's tuition. Many chefs feel that cooking schools are a waste of time. They believe that an apprenticeship is much more useful. Wendy disagrees, holding that there are advantages to learning about cuisine in the center of cuisine.

Besides teaching technique, the school offered a ticket to the back doors of three-star restaurants in Paris. Students were expected to work and observe the French *brigade de cuisine* (kitchen staff) in action. The kitchen of a French restaurant is divided into several positions, or stations, each producing a different part of the meal. The head chef holds all the parts together. Varying according to an establishment's size, the kitchen staff would consist of a *chef saucier* (sauce chef), who is second in command; an *entremettier*, in charge of soups and vegetables; a *garde-manger* (larder chef), who, among other duties, manages the supplies; and a *rôtisseur*, who prepares the roasts and grilled dishes. As the restaurant grows so do the size and degree of specialization of each station.

"If I had to evaluate what Paris did for me," said Wendy, "I'd say it gave me a tool to evaluate what we're doing here in America; it gave me a way to judge things. If you work five or six days a week, you don't get the chance to get out and try things." Currently, she works at least fifty hours a week.

Anne, Wendy's junior by seven years, also went to the University of California at Santa Barbara. She worked one Christmas break for Ranch kitchen staff who wanted the day off. In her spare time, she went through recipe books, making all kinds of pastries. Pastries became an abiding interest. She dropped out of college because she thought the kitchen offered a better education. During 1978, she taught herself, "by the book, Julia Child all the way." Her tenacity paid off in the following year when Wendy hired her as pastry chef.

How do the two of them work together? What about the pressure, the heat, the constant deadlines of restaurant work? "Most of the time it's wonderful. But we can take it out on each other. Wendy expects more work out of me than she does of a normal employee," says Anne. "It's great. I like working with her. We rarely have words," says Wendy. There are, however, occasional rough spots. The Napoleon Caper was one. "That was our last fight," says Anne, who hates to make Napoleons (also called *milles-feuilles*) because they are "something from the sixties." Wendy concurs that it's like "being asked to make a hamburger every night." But the waiters reported that customers kept asking for Napoleons. Wendy urged Anne to continue making them. Anne refused.

After more than one argument, Wendy read the ultimatum: "Close your eyes, grit your teeth, and make a Napoleon every night." The executive chef had spoken. The pastry chef obeyed, the waiters were relieved, and the Napoleon-coveting customers enjoyed their dessert, not caring a bit that they were out of fashion.

CHANTERELLE SALAD

Chanterelles grow in the Santa Ynez mountains after about a week of rains in November or December. The longer the rainy season, the more chanterelle mushrooms we have. As the season progresses, the number of vendors increases and the price goes down to around $3.00 a pound. My sister and her husband have braved the poison oak to find chanterelles on Ranch property. They grow under oak trees and under the fallen oak leaf cover. There is really nothing quite so good as the meaty, intense flavor of a chanterelle mushroom. I prefer the smaller mushroom, but only for aesthetic reasons. A large chanterelle, chopped finely, makes a good cream of mushroom soup.

FOR THE SALAD

Look for the freshest of bitter greens and allow 1 cup, loosely packed, per person. I favor greens such as chicory (curly endive), *arugula*, Belgian endive, spinach, and watercress. Wash and pick through a mixture of greens. Dry them in a tea towel and store in the refrigerator.

MARINADE/DRESSING

1 cup good olive oil
⅓ cup raspberry vinegar
2 shallots, finely chopped
2 tablespoons lemon juice
Salt and freshly ground pepper to taste

Mix all the ingredients together. Reserve half for the greens and the other half for a marinade.

CHANTERELLES

Clean and pick over the fresh chanterelles (allowing about ¼ pound per person) and then slice the mushrooms, if necessary, so that they are all approximately the same size. Pour the reserved marinade over the mushrooms and let them sit for half an hour.

Cook the mushrooms over charcoal or mesquite, under the flame of a broiler, or in a sauté pan until they are done, about 5 minutes. While they are still hot, mix them with the greens and the raspberry vinegar dressing. Serve immediately with goat cheese, croutons, and toasted pine nuts.

VARIATION
Instead of the goat cheese, etcetera, add warm shredded duck meat or smoked duck meat to the salad.

# STEAMED MUSSELS
WITH ARTICHOKES

In Santa Barbara we have a local company that harvests mussels grown at least five miles offshore. These shellfish are not affected by the red tide and so are exempt from the usual May-through-August quarantine. They are so fresh that they will keep for up to seven days in the refrigerator if iced down and not de-bearded.

For an appetizer, I allow between eight and ten mussels per person; for an entrée, I would double that quantity. At The Plow and Angel we serve a different mussel appetizer every night and I have a large collection of recipes for them. Mussels may be prepared in a number of ways. They are usually steamed open first and then: served chilled on the half shell; skewered and broiled over mesquite; served with a cream sauce made with the white wine in which they were steamed; or the meat may be removed and stuffed into artichoke bottoms or tomato halves.

8 to 10 mussels per person (16 to 20 if the dish is to be
*   served as a first course, not an appetizer)*
2 scant cups white wine
4 shallots, minced
1 clove garlic, minced
1½ cups heavy cream
3 cooked artichoke bottoms, cut into small wedges
3 tablespoons minced chives and/or 3 teaspoons fresh thyme
3 tablespoons Dijon mustard
Salt, pepper, and lemon juice to taste

To clean the mussels, scrub them under cold running water and pull off their beards. They should not be de-bearded until immediately before they are to be used (within 10 to 15 minutes) because they should be cooked live and de-bearding will kill them.

Steam the mussels in the white wine over a high flame until they have just opened. Remove the mussels from the pan and reserve, covered, in a warm place while the sauce is being made.

Return the cooking liquids to the flame and add the shallots, garlic, and cream. Reduce the cream slightly and add the artichokes and herbs. Whisk in the Dijon mustard to thicken the sauce and adjust the seasoning with salt, pepper, and lemon juice.

Arrange the mussels in individual heated bowls and nap with the finished sauce. Serve at once, with plenty of sourdough bread.

 ABALONE AMANDINE

ABALONE WITH ALMONDS

I buy abalone that has already been processed by a local fish company. All it needs is a little more pounding with the flat side of an aluminum or wooden mallet to make it ready to cook.

I always serve abalone sautéed dorée*: that is, dipped in flour, then in beaten egg. I then sauté the abalone over very high heat in clarified butter for about ten seconds on each side. These details are very important. If the butter is not clarified, it will burn before it becomes hot enough (clarified butter has the highest smoking point of any cooking oil); if the pan is not smoking hot, the abalone will be tough.*

I generally offer abalone with some type of beurre blanc *and a garnish that adds a crunchy texture.*

8 small pieces abalone, each weighing about ½ ounce
Salt and pepper
About 1 cup flour
1 egg, beaten
4 tablespoons raw slivered almonds

Season the abalone with the salt and pepper, dust lightly with some of the flour, dip into the beaten egg, and then into a light mixture of the slivered almonds combined with no more than 6 tablespoons of flour.

Sauté the coated abalone in clarified butter over a high heat for about 10 seconds on each side. Place on a heated plate and nap with the chive and butter sauce.

BEURRE BLANC AUX CIBOULETTES

CHIVE-BUTTER SAUCE

2 shallots, finely chopped
⅓ cup white wine
Juice of half a lemon
2 tablespoons heavy cream
1 cup butter, cold, and cut into pieces
Salt and white pepper, to taste
2 tablespoons minced chives

Combine the shallots, wine, and lemon juice in a stainless steel pan. Reduce over a moderate heat until only about 2 tablespoons remain. Add the cream and reduce again until the sauce is thick. Do not let the sauce at the bottom of the pan brown. Now, with the pan still over the heat, whisk in the cold butter in small batches to make a smooth, creamy sauce. Finish the sauce with salt, pepper, and the chopped chives.

This sauce may be made ahead of time and kept warm.

 # FRESH PLUM SORBET

Everything I cook is made from scratch.

2 pounds plums
1⅓ cups sugar syrup (recipe below)
Juice of 1 lemon

Using only the ripest plums for the best flavor, blanch and skin the fruit by dropping them briefly into boiling water and then running cold water over them. The skins should fall off easily. Extract the pits and purée the flesh in a blender. Press the purée through a fine mesh sieve to remove fibers and strings. Stir in the lemon juice and sugar syrup. Freeze in an ice cream machine for 20 to 30 minutes or until set.

SUGAR SYRUP
2½ cups sugar
2 cups plus 2 tablespoons water

Combine the sugar and water in a saucepan. Place over high heat and stir to dissolve the sugar crystals. Bring to a full boil. Remove from the heat and pour the syrup into a clean bowl. Cool completely before using. Covered, this syrup can be kept indefinitely in the refrigerator.

*Fresh raspberries are hard to come by except for two short months out of twelve,
so I change the fruit seasonally, using blueberries, strawberries, peaches, or kiwis.
All are beautiful garnishes for the pale yellow tart. For the shell I use a* pâte su-
crée *(recipe in any good cookbook), which is crisp and delicate. Cook the shell
completely and, as soon as it is removed from the oven, brush with egg white
whisked with a pinch of salt; this provides a glazed, moisture-proof seal between
the pastry and the filling.*

LEMON BUTTER FILLING
5 egg yolks
½ cup sugar
¼ cup fresh lemon juice
Finely grated rind of 1 lemon
5 tablespoons unsalted butter, softened

In the top of a double boiler, whisk together the egg yolks, sugar, lemon
juice, and rind. Whisk constantly over medium-high heat until mixture becomes foamy and starts to resemble softly whipped cream. Whisk in the
butter, 1 tablespoon at a time. Keep whisking until the mixture thickens.
This should take between 10 and 15 minutes altogether. Remove from heat.
Pour the lemon filling into the tart shell and cover closely with plastic wrap
to prevent a skin from forming. Refrigerate until thoroughly chilled. Garnish with whipped cream and fresh raspberries.

Cindy Pawlcyn

CINDY PAWLCYN

MUSTARDS · SAINT HELENA
RIO GRILL · CARMEL
FOG CITY DINER · SAN FRANCISCO

CINDY PAWLCYN is a diminutive fireball, whose three restaurants in Northern California keep both critics and customers coming back for more Americana. In a little over four years, Cindy and her three partners, Bill Higgins, Bill Upson, and Bill Cox, have established their company, Real Restaurants, as a moving force in Bay Area dining. Their first enterprise was Mustards Grill in the Napa Valley; then came the Rio Grill in Carmel, followed by the Fog City Diner in San Francisco. From the beginning the partners had wanted an establishment in the city by the bay, but the cost of space was too high. With the company's success, that no longer seems to be a problem.

"The food is very approachable, very honest," said Jan Weimer, the food editor of *Bon Appétit*. Cindy "uses a lot of grilling, and a lot of smoking. Her cooking style is a lot less trendy than what many others are doing." Cindy herself describes it as "pretty straightforward. People can understand it and enjoy it. I don't like involved food. Food should be made to be enjoyed." Typical *à la carte* selections include small plates, grilled items, and salads, allowing opportunity for grazing. Cindy was "grazing" at the family dinner table long before anyone had invented the term. Dinner for the four children—she is the youngest by six years—always meant a variety of food. She acquired her Norwegian and German tastes from her mother and her Russian tastes from her father.

As Cindy's interest in cooking developed, her mother encouraged her to attend professional food classes. By the time she was in high school she was working five nights a week for a local kitchen equipment and catering company. Verna Meyers, the Cordon Bleu–trained chef who ran the cooking school, and Lois Lee, who owned the equipment store, convinced Cindy that she, too, could be a chef. After finishing high school, she entered the chefs' program at Hennepin Technical Institute and then moved on to the University of Wisconsin, in Stout. She graduated with honors from the hotel and restaurant administration program and went on to Chicago to learn something about *nouvelle cuisine* from a Spanish chef. While she was working as the *sous chef* at the Pump Room, a hotel restaurant well known in Chicago, she met two of the three Bills who are now her partners. Within a month of leaving Chicago for California, they asked her to join them.

Mustards opened in 1983, the Rio Grill six months later, and Fog City Diner in 1985. With three restaurants, Cindy is constantly traveling. She spends two days a week at each restaurant, and has a separate bag packed for each place. "I can't ever find anything at home," she said. "Between my husband and my housekeeper, they keep me confused. Where'd you put the garbage bags this week? At the restaurants I know where everything is."

Her diligent touring—undertaken also by her partners on occasion—has saved Cindy from the most hazardous pitfall in owning several restaurants: Usually, as a chef expands, quality will suffer in the old restaurant, the new, or both. One key element is that the resident chefs have all been with her since the restaurants opened, a stability unusual in the transitory world of restaurant kitchens.

When not traveling to her various restaurants, Pawlcyn is on the road traveling for pleasure, to England, southern Europe, Asia, or back home to Chicago to eat in her favorite restaurant, Les Nomads. "But, let's face it, if I'm sitting in Italy and they are shaving white truffles, I want to get back to [one of my] kitchens and play with [truffles, too]," she said.

This soup is really clean and flavorful. It is a wonderful way to start a meal because it's so bright, such a marvelous color, especially in the summertime.

1 quart buttermilk
1 cup chicken stock
1 cup sour cream
1½ tablespoons sugar
½ teaspoon Dijon mustard
1 tablespoon red wine vinegar
4 pounds cooked and peeled beets
3 English cucumbers, peeled, seeded, and chopped
3 green onions, minced
Salt and white pepper to taste

GARNISH
Chopped English cucumber
Sour cream
Sprigs of dill

Combine all the ingredients, except those for the garnish, in a food processor and blend until smooth. Thin the soup with chicken stock if necessary. Sieve the mixture into a bowl and chill.

Serve garnished with the extra chopped cucumber and sour cream and about 3 to 6 sprigs of dill.

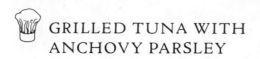

GRILLED TUNA WITH ANCHOVY PARSLEY

I like this because there is a flavor-burst inside. As you are eating it, you get different amounts of the anchovy paste in different bites. The saltiness contrasts with the meat.

2½ pounds fresh tuna (approximately 6 to 7 ounces per
    serving)
3 cloves garlic, peeled and mashed
2 tablespoons Italian parsley, chopped
1 tablespoon fresh rosemary, minced
1 or 2 anchovy fillets
1 tablespoon virgin olive oil

Cut the tuna into steaks about 1½ to 2 inches thick. (The quality of the tuna is most important as it should be cooked quickly and served medium-rare.)

Make a paste of the rest of the ingredients. Slit the tuna steaks in 4 or 5 places with the tip of a small paring knife and insert a small amount of paste into each slit. Brush the steaks lightly with olive oil and grill them over hot coals for approximately 2 minutes on each side. The steaks may also be sautéed in a cast-iron pan over medium heat.

Serve with Warm Tomato and Pepper Salsa.

WARM TOMATO & PEPPER SALSA

This salsa is moist and juicy, especially when the tomatoes are ripe. Sun-ripened tomatoes are the best to use, especially in the summer when they smell, taste, and feel like real tomatoes.

3 tablespoons butter
½ cup leeks, thinly sliced
Half a medium-sized red bell pepper, cut en julienne
Half a medium-sized, fresh pasilla chili, cut en julienne
½ cup tomato, concassé (i.e., peeled, seeded, and chopped)
Salt and white pepper
Pinches of fresh Italian parsley and rosemary, chopped fine
¼ cup Niçoise olives

Heat the butter in a large saucepan and, when it begins to bubble, add the leeks. Sauté for 1 minute. Add the pepper and the chili, and cook for 2 minutes. Add the tomato *concassé* and herbs, salt, and pepper to taste. Simmer until heated through. Add the olives and serve as an accompaniment to the tuna.

SPICED GRILLED MARINATED POUSSIN

This dish has all sorts of different flavors when you bite into it because of the marinade, which keeps the birds juicy.

8 medium-sized cloves of garlic, peeled and roughly chopped
3 scallions, roughly chopped
1 piece fresh lemon grass, about 1½ inches long, minced
1 piece fresh ginger, about 1½ inches long, peeled and
    minced
1 chipotle *chili*
½ oz. black bean paste with chilies
2 tablespoons Anaheim (or any mild, red, unblended) chili
    powder
½ cup rice vinegar
½ cup olive or peanut oil
Half a bunch of cilantro

6 poussin (chicken or quail may be substituted)

Make the marinade by combining in a food processor the garlic, scallions, lemon grass, ginger, chili, black bean paste, and chili powder. Chop finely. While the machine is running, add the rice vinegar, oil, and cilantro. Set aside.

Wipe the birds and remove their backbones. Press the breastbones to lie flat and tuck the wing tips behind the shoulders. Make a slit in the lower portion of the breast skin and tuck the first (bottom) knuckle of the legs into the hole, or tie the legs together with string around the bottom knuckles. The birds should now somewhat resemble frogs.

Spread the marinade liberally on both sides of each bird and allow them to marinate for 24 hours in the refrigerator.

108 · CINDY PAWLCYN

Make a charcoal or wood fire—low in flame, with a strong coal base. Cook the birds, bone-side down, slowly, for 15 to 20 minutes, finishing skin-side down. Or, roast the birds in a 425°F oven until the juices run clear, about 25 to 30 minutes.

Serve with grilled and peeled sweet bell peppers, grilled sweetcorn, and Mango and Cucumber Relish.

MANGO & CUCUMBER RELISH

This relish has a nice contrast of both texture and taste, like Indian food. The combination of a crispy bird hot off the grill and a cold relish is dynamite. It may also be used with plain barbecued poultry or with fish.

1 cucumber, peeled, seeded, and minced
2 large mangoes (or 1 papaya), peeled and minced
1 scallion, de-rooted and minced
1 teaspoon cayenne pepper
2 tablespoons rice vinegar
1 tablespoon avocado or peanut oil
Pinches of salt and freshly ground white pepper
2 or 3 tablespoons fresh sweet or opal basil (dried basil is no
     substitute; instead use fresh chives or tarragon)

Combine all the ingredients and serve with the grilled poussin.

Annie Somerville

ANNIE SOMERVILLE
GREENS · SAN FRANCISCO

GREENS, the landmark vegetarian restaurant in San Francisco, began as "a place for people to work who were practicing Buddhism at the Zen Center," says Annie Somerville, who is now executive chef. She oversees a staff of thirty as well as plans and cooks the weekend *prix fixe* dinner for the 125-seat restaurant. Although Greens is still owned by the San Francisco Zen Center, it has evolved over its eight-year existence to include many cooks who have nothing to do with Zen. Also, says Annie, only a small percentage of the clientele is actually vegetarian.

The restaurant's wide appeal is, in part, because of the modest prices, but it's mostly due to the tempting food. Anyone who has tasted standard meatless fare knows that to keep vegetarian cooking interesting is indeed a challenge.

"Over the years we have developed at Greens a vegetarian cuisine, using vegetables in season and the best quality ingredients we can get. We emphasize taste, form, and presentation. We try to present food at its simplest. We are not a health food restaurant but we think about how much butter and how much oil we use. Because we have to create every dish from vegetables, we have the most fun creating menus in summer," she says.

When Annie is planning her five-course *prix fixe* dinners, she enjoys thinking up the appetizers most. On one Saturday night, the restaurant served a Sonoma goat cheese that had been rolled in bread crumbs, baked, and then presented on a bed of Blue Lake green beans, with golden and Chioggia beets that were marinated in a lemon and tarragon vinaigrette.

Cherry tomatoes (the 'Sweet 100' variety) and yellow pear tomatoes decorated the platter. Whenever Annie talks about vegetables, she gets that specific—it's never just tomatoes, but always the particular variety, the ripeness, the taste.

She has been the executive chef for two years, since Deborah Madison, who had been the founding chef, left the restaurant to go to Italy. Annie seems almost surprised by her own success. "I never realized that I would be the chef of this complex an organization," she says.

Her first professional involvement with food began at the Tassajara Zen Center, which is at the site of an old spa that the San Francisco Zen Center purchased in 1967. The springs lie at the end of fourteen miles of dirt road, a three-hour drive from the city. Tassajara accepts guests during the summer. For the rest of the year, it is closed to the public, and students and their teachers practice the Japanese *soto* style of Zen Buddhism.

Annie began as a student at the Center in 1973. In 1975 she began living there and working in the kitchen. She graduated from the kitchen crew, to assistant cook, to summer guest cook, to head cook in two years. "We cooked much simpler food [at Tassajara] than we do here at the restaurant," she says. "There was a spirit of working together, which is still alive at Greens now."

She left the kitchen to run the Center's stitchery store, Alaya, in San Francisco. Alaya sold, among other things, meditation pillows and Japanese bedding. When the Center sold the store, Annie moved to Greens to become assistant lunch chef. Again, she worked her way up the ladder. Although many of the original members have left, the restaurant's structure is still based on traditional ideas. Every part of life at the Zen Center is hierarchical. "When Deborah Madison left, replacements were made from within. It never occurred to anyone to hire a professional from outside."

Will Annie, who is no longer a practicing member of the Center, stay with her alma mater? "Absolutely! It's a unique spot. There is something very particular for me there."

To would-be chefs she says, "I would caution anyone to be sure that this is really what you want to do. The role of chef looks glamorous, but it is a lot of hard work that requires loads of dedication. The keys to a restaurant's success are creativity and stability. If one overpowers the other, you get into trouble. You need balance to find a system that works."

MEXICAN LENTIL SOUP WITH ROASTED GARLIC & LIME

SERVES FOUR
TO SIX

This is a delicious and spicy soup. The roasted garlic gives it depth and richness and the chilpotle chilies add a little heat.

TOMATO STOCK
1 medium yellow onion
1 small head garlic
2 carrots, peeled
1 zucchini
½ pound mushrooms
3 medium tomatoes
1 medium potato
1 teaspoon salt
A handful of fresh herbs: parsley, thyme, oregano
2 bay leaves
8 cups cold water

SOUP
1 cup lentils, cleaned and rinsed
1 bay leaf
2 heads garlic
2 tablespoons olive oil
1 medium red onion, diced
2 cloves garlic, finely chopped
1 teaspoon salt
1 carrot, diced
1 medium red pepper, diced
1 medium yellow or green pepper, diced
2 teaspoons cumin seed

1 teaspoon dried oregano
1 to 2 teaspoons chilpotle *chilies, puréed or minced*
¼ cup lime juice
1 bunch cilantro, chopped

To make about 6 cups of stock, chop the vegetables, add salt, fresh herbs, and bay leaves. Cover with cold water, bring to a boil, and turn down to a simmer. Simmer for up to 1 hour, strain stock, and set aside.

Cover the lentils with cold water, add the bay leaf, and cook until tender, about 30 minutes.

To roast the garlic, heat the oven to 350°F. Slice the tops off the 2 heads of garlic. Place in a shallow baking dish, brush with olive oil, cover and bake until tender, about 30 minutes. Be sure that the garlic does not burn. When the garlic cools, squeeze it from the heads, and purée with a little of the stock.

Heat the 2 tablespoons olive oil in a soup pot and add the onions, chopped garlic, and salt. When the onions begin to melt, add the carrots and peppers. While the vegetables are cooking, toast the cumin seeds and oregano in a dry skillet over medium heat just until they begin to release their aroma. Cool and grind in a spice mill or pestle and mortar. Add to the cooking vegetables.

When the vegetables are tender, add the cooked lentils in their broth and enough tomato stock to reach the desired consistency. The soup should not be too thick. Add the roasted garlic and the *chilpotle* purée to taste. Finish seasoning the soup with lime juice and more salt if necessary. Garnish with chopped cilantro.

GRILLED POTATO SALAD WITH SUMMER VEGETABLES

This salad is a delicious way to enjoy potatoes. Although it is not essential, grilling the potatoes gives them additional flavor and crispness.

2 pounds assorted small potatoes
3 tablespoons olive oil
$\frac{1}{2}$ teaspoon salt
A few pinches of freshly ground pepper
1 small head garlic
$\frac{1}{2}$ pound Blue Lake green beans
$\frac{1}{2}$ pound yellow wax beans
1 medium red pepper
1 medium yellow pepper
1 small red onion
1 bunch Italian parsley
A small handful of Niçoise olives

VINAIGRETTE
2 tablespoons lemon juice
The zest of 1 lemon
1 tablespoon sherry vinegar
2 small cloves garlic, finely chopped
6 tablespoons olive oil
1 small bunch basil, chopped

Prepare your grill with mesquite or charcoal. Heat the oven to 400°F for roasting the potatoes. Toss the washed potatoes with the olive oil, salt, pepper, and a few cloves of unpeeled garlic. Bake until tender; about 30 to 40 minutes.

While the potatoes are baking, prepare the vegetables and make the vinaigrette. Blanch the beans in boiling salted water for 1 minute. They should be crisp and bright, but not raw. Thinly slice the peppers and onions.

Cut the baked potatoes in half and skewer them for grilling. (If you do not have a grill, the potatoes can be broiled.) Grill the potatoes until crisp and golden; about 5 minutes. Remove the potatoes from the skewers and toss them with the peppers, beans, and onions in the vinaigrette. Season with more sherry vinegar, salt, and pepper if necessary. Garnish with Niçoise olives and sprigs of Italian parsley.

WILTED SPINACH SALAD WITH ROASTED PEPPERS

This salad is a wonderful variation on the Greens spinach salad with feta cheese.

1 large bunch spinach
1 small head escarole or frisée (a French curly endive)
8 slices French baguette, each ½-inch thick
1 large red or yellow pepper roasted, peeled, and sliced into
    julienne strips
5 tablespoons olive oil
2 tablespoons balsamic vinegar
1 clove garlic, finely chopped
2 pinches salt
1 pinch freshly ground black pepper
3 ounces grated Parmesan cheese (preferably Parmigiano
    Reggiano)
A small handful of thinly sliced red onion
12 pitted Niçoise olives

Heat the oven to 375°F. Prepare the spinach and escarole or *frisée* by discarding the tough outer leaves and stems. Wash and spin dry. Brush baguette slices with olive oil and bake for 5 to 7 minutes, until crisp. Season the roasted pepper strips with a little of the olive oil, balsamic vinegar, garlic, salt, and pepper.

Combine all the ingredients except the olive oil in a large bowl. Heat the olive oil in a small skillet until it is very hot, but not smoking. Pour the heated oil over the salad and toss so that it coats and wilts the leaves. Season the salad with more vinegar, salt, and pepper if necessary.

SNAPSHOTS

SANDRA MARIA BAZABAL
Mount Signal Café · Calexico

The Mount Signal Café might be something out of a Sam Shepherd play. "On a quiet remote corner of State 98, there is a cluster of faded buildings, barking dogs, and a couple of rusting gasoline pumps. The scene is reminiscent of wayside shops advertising your 'Last chance to fill up for fifty miles.'"

But the Mount Signal Café, eight miles west of Calexico and named for the 2,262-foot high mountain to the south, is not "lost in the middle of nowhere." It has achieved so much fame that people often come from San Diego, a drive of more than two hours, to enjoy one of Sandra Bazabal's combination plates. Pheasant hunters come in droves during the fall, farmers from throughout the Imperial Valley arrive in their trucks. The Blue Angels feast there often, and have hung autographed pictures on the dark interior walls.

Bullfighters come up from Mexicali, Mexico, and add their likenesses to the posters and portraits cluttered behind the bar. César Pastor visited Mount Signal before his fight in the Calafia ring. His poise and carriage, his charisma if you will, made all heads turn as he entered the restau-

Sandra Maria Bazabal

rant. It was not until he greeted Sandra Maria that many patrons recognized in her the same elegant stance. Before becoming a chef, she was a bullfighter.

Sandra Maria Jésus Bazabal was born in Guadalajara, Mexico, in 1929. She went to school there and at the age of eight, began her lifelong affair with the bulls. When she was twelve, she met Conchita Cintron, the famous bullfighter, who has always served as a role model for her, *la mejor*, a woman who merited all her respect. One highlight of Sandra Maria's bullfighting career came in 1946 when she was one of six women who fought alongside the renowned actor and comedian, Cantinflas, in the bullring of Mexico city.

Two years later, she moved to the United States to Calexico, "to find a new life." Ten years after that, she and her new husband opened the Mount Signal Café. Juan Bautista Bazabal, a Basque, moved to the Imperial Valley in 1936, where he started as a shepherd. In 1957, he and his wife purchased the restaurant site. A schoolhouse that had stood there had burned down the year before. Juan Bautista died in 1979, leaving behind two sons in the U.S. Navy and a daughter.

Sandra Maria began as the chef at Mount Signal and now runs the entire, successful operation. She learned to cook at home in Guadalajara, and honed her skills as chef in a boarding house for medical students there. Today, three of her sisters—Esperanze Canes, Lupe Villa, and Rosa Vasquez—help her in the kitchen, and a friend, Mika Torres, helps her out front.

CHIMICHANGAS ESTILO SONORA

SONORAN-STYLE ROLLED TACOS

SERVES SIX

A chimichanga is a filled, deep-fried flour tortilla.

3 pounds beef short ribs
2 large, ripe tomatoes, diced
1 medium onion, diced
2 fresh chiles pasillas, *seeded and diced*
12 wheat tortillas
1 pound Monterey Jack cheese, cut into
    thin strips

GARNISH
½ cup heavy cream
½ cup guacamole

Boil the meat, in salted water or stock to cover, until tender. Allow to cool. Remove the flesh from the bones and shred. Make a *picadillo* by sautéing the meat in some of its cooking broth with the tomatoes, onion, and *chiles*.

Fill each tortilla with some *picadillo* and a strip of cheese and roll it up. Fry them in pork lard or vegetable oil, until crisp but not hard.

Serve in pairs with a line of heavy cream and another of *guacamole* poured over each.

CAROL BRENDLINGER
Bay Wolf Restaurant • Oakland

"As the oldest of seven children, I started cooking very early in my life. While studying architecture at U.C. Berkeley, cooking became a hobby when I lived in various shared houses and everyone took turns cooking dinner. I read cookbooks for bedtime stories when I was sick of studying physics.

"My first job cooking came about in an odd way. Paolo Soleri brought his exhibit of plans for a solar city in Arizona to the museum at the University. I thought I would like to learn solar design and concrete construction from him, but could not afford the fees. I found out he needed a camp cook, so I thought I could earn a living and learn construction at the same time. As a result, I read the *Joy of Cooking* from cover to cover, multiplied everything by twenty, and ended up cooking three meals a day for one hundred and ten people in a kitchen with no air conditioning in the middle of the desert. I never did learn concrete construction, but I learned a lot about running a kitchen.

"When I came back to the Bay Area, I ran a small café for a while (making soups and salads). I then started at the Bay Wolf, making

Carol Brendlinger

salads. I have been here ever since (eight years), advancing through all the work stations and I am now the *chef de cuisine*. I also teach classes and write recipes for magazines and books.

"As a result of my previous backgrounds, and the myriad ethnic influences of California, I tend to take a scholarly, but improvisitory, approach to recipe development. I love to go back to the roots of a cuisine, study the historical and social influences on the cultures involved, and pick out the basic forms and essences. Then I do what any modern practitioner of *nouvelle cuisine* would do—lighten the recipes for contemporary appetites, i.e., reduce the fats and sugars and use the freshest ingredients available. In short—create something."

SMOKED DUCK BREAST WITH PEARS & PERSIMMONS

SERVES SIX

3 firm pears
3 Fuyu (Japanese) persimmons
3 tablespoons lemon juice
6 smoked duck breasts, skin removed
6 tablespoons butter
2 tablespoons fresh ginger, minced

Peel, core, and slice the fruit lengthwise. Toss the slices with the lemon juice to keep them from darkening.

Slice the duck breasts thinly lengthwise and arrange in fan shapes on 6 plates.

Melt the butter in a large frying pan. Add the ginger and simmer on medium heat for 1 minute. Add the fruit and any liquid. Turn the heat to high and toss the fruit gently until it's just heated through. Put the fruit and juices next to the duck on the plates. Serve immediately.

BIBA CAGGIANO
Biba • Sacramento

Born and raised in Bologna, Italy's gastronomical capital, Biba Caggiano comes from an old Bolognese family in which she grew up cooking the classic food of her native Emilia-Romagna region. In 1960 Biba married Dr. Vincent Caggiano while he was attending Bologna's faculty of medicine, and moved to New York, his home town. In 1970, she and her family moved to Sacramento, California. Discovering the lack of authentic Italian food there—the subtle and inventive regional cooking was nowhere to be seen—she set out to do something about it.

During her trips home, Biba collected recipes and learned everything she could about the culinary traditions of Italy—knowledge she has been sharing with others in cooking classes in California, Oregon, and Washington as well as in classes in Bologna itself, where she was the only guest teacher at the Marcella Hazan Cooking School. Biba also joined the California Culinary Academy as a guest teacher and a lecturer.

In 1978 she was asked to do a weekly segment on an evening television magazine called "Weeknight." Then the station sent Biba back to

Biba Caggiano

Bologna with a film crew to produce a nightly two-week series on location. The response was incredible; forty thousand requests for recipes were received. Biba remained as the station's resident chef until the magazine went off the air in 1986. Her cooking abilities and sense of humor put her

125

on television shows all over the country, from Los Angeles to New York, reaching a national television audience via the Hearst-ABC cable service "Daytime Show" and VTV (Value Television).

Biba is the author of two books on Italian food: *Northern Italian Cooking*, published by HP Books, and *Modern Italian Cooking*, published by Simon and Schuster.

In August 1986, the restaurant Biba was opened. Only five months after she opened, Biba received, from the restaurant reviewer of the *Sacramento Bee*, three and a half stars, the highest award ever given in Sacramento.

. . .

RISOTTO CON LA MENTUCCIA

RISOTTO WITH MINT

SERVES FOUR TO SIX

6 cups homemade chicken broth or 3
    cups canned broth mixed with 3 cups
    water
5 tablespoons unsalted butter
1 onion, finely chopped
2 cups Italian Arborio rice
1 cup dry white wine
⅓ cup loosely packed fresh mint leaves
1 cup freshly grated Parmesan cheese
Salt to taste

Heat the broth in a medium-sized saucepan and keep it warm over very low heat.

Melt 4 tablespoons of the butter in a large saucepan. When the butter foams, add the onion. Sauté over medium heat until the onion is pale yellow. Add the rice. Cook for 1 to 2 minutes, or just enough to coat the rice with the butter and onion. Stir in the wine. Cook, stirring constantly, until the wine has evaporated. Add a few ladles of broth, just enough barely to cover the rice. Cook over medium heat, until broth has been absorbed.

Continue cooking and stirring the rice in this manner, adding broth a bit at a time, until the rice is done, 15 to 20 minutes. During the last 2 or 3 minutes of cooking, chop the mint very fine and add to the rice with the remaining tablespoon of butter and ⅓ cup of the Parmesan cheese. Taste for seasoning and doneness. The rice should be tender but still firm to the bite. At this point, the rice should have a creamy, moist consistency.

Serve immediately with the remaining Parmesan cheese. As a first course, this recipe will serve 6 people; as a main course with salad, it will serve 4.

CECILIA CHIANG
The Mandarin • San Francisco & Beverly Hills

"My first restaurant was in Tokyo. I took the last plane from Shanghai to Japan with my family in 1949, and we started the restaurant in 1950 with my cousin because we were so hungry for good Chinese food. I didn't even know how to cook. We hired cooks from Hong Kong, who had been trained on the mainland.

"In 1958 I came to San Francisco to visit my sister. Chinese restaurants were then serving *egg foo yung* and *chow mein*. I looked at a menu and said, 'What are all these dishes that I've never heard of before?' And I thought, 'This is just awful. Most Americans must think that all Chinese food is like that.' So I decided to start a restaurant here. The first one was on Polk Street. It was really a little restaurant—what you would call a joint. But we served real Chinese food. It was hard at first. People would walk in and say, 'No egg roll, no *chop suey*, what is this?'

"One thing I think about Chinese restaurants is that the competition is very keen. Much more than before. Before, people were happy with mediocre dishes. Now they know the difference. They've traveled and been to

Cecilia Chiang

different places. I think people are now starting to learn—really learn—about Chinese food."

127

MINCED SQUAB

SERVES TWO TO FOUR

12 dried Chinese black mushrooms
2 large squab
1 cup water chestnuts
1 cup rice noodles (available from Asian
    grocers)
3 cups plus 4 tablespoons vegetable oil
1 large tomato
1 head iceberg lettuce
2 scallions (white parts only), minced
2 teaspoons minced Virginia ham
1 teaspoon fresh ginger, peeled and
    minced
1 tablespoon rice wine or dry sherry
1 tablespoon oyster sauce
1 tablespoon soy sauce
½ teaspoon sesame seed oil
½ teaspoon sugar
¼ teaspoon pepper

Soak the black mushrooms in warm water for approximately 20 minutes.

While waiting for the mushrooms to soften, bone the squab and chop the meat, with the skin left on, into small pieces. Squeeze out the water from the softened mushrooms, discard the stems, and chop the mushrooms and the water chestnuts.

Deep fry the rice noodles in the 3 cups of oil that have been warmed, but not allowed to get much hotter than 270°F. Allow them to cool, and then crumble them and spread them out onto a serving platter. These noodles puff up almost instantly as soon as they are in the oil, so be prepared to remove them within seconds.

Cut the tomato into wedges and scoop out the flesh. Arrange the wedges around the edge of the serving platter.

Remove between 8 and 12 leaves from the head of lettuce and trim their edges to form lettuce-leaf cups. So as to provide a greater contrast with the lightly spiced squab, chill these cups in the refrigerator.

Heat the remaining 4 tablespoons of oil in a wok until hot. Add the squab with the chopped scallions and stir fry for 30 seconds. Add the mushrooms, water chestnuts, ham, ginger, and seasonings and continue to stir fry for another 2 minutes. Mound the squab mixture over the noodles.

To serve, the noodles and squab are spooned into the lettuce cups, which are garnished with tomato wedges, and eaten with the fingers.

NOTE

If squab is considered too rich and oily, a mixture of chicken and squab may be substituted.

BARBARA FIGUEROA
Camelions • Santa Monica

The culinary adventures of Barbara Figueroa, a native of New York, began in James Beard's cooking classes. Following his advice, she enrolled in the hotel and restaurant program at New York City Technical College. While earning her degree, she became only the second woman that the school had ever sent abroad to study with a French chef. That apprenticeship in Gascony at André Daguin's two-star Hôtel de France in Auch was, she says, a revelation; never before had she worked with products brought from local farms only minutes away. What a difference it made!

Barbara Figueroa

Her standards several notches higher by the time she graduated, she sought and found work in such Manhattan restaurants as Le Cirque, Restaurant Maurice, and Jams. She is presently one of the chefs at Camelions in Santa Monica. In addition, she directs and cooks at various functions, including those held by the Chaîne des Rôtisseurs and the American Institute of Wine and Food.

She also writes. She is a contributing editor for *Gastronome*, the publication of the Chaîne des Rôtisseurs, and a free-lance writer for several other magazines and newspapers. In 1986 she was collaborating with Wolfgang Puck in the writing of his second cookbook. "We'd get up early and spend hours knocking back *espressos* and working away at the manuscript. Then we'd swing right into preparation for the evening service at the restaurant. It was hectic. But listening to Wolf's history was so fascinating. Besides, he's a great yarn-spinner; we practically laughed our way through the entire book!"

FOIE GRAS WITH FIGS & PISTACHIO NUTS

SERVES FOUR

2 dried Calmyrna figs (white figs), diced
1 tablespoon finely chopped shallots
½ cup brown veal stock
2 tablespoons medium-dry Madeira
3½ tablespoons ruby port
4 tablespoons butter
½ cup chicken stock
3 tablespoons shelled, unsalted pistachio
    nuts
4 medium or 6 small ripe, but slightly
    firm fresh figs (Calmyrna, Mission, or
    other variety)
14 ounces fresh foie gras, cut into 4
    uniform slices, each about ½ inch
    thick
2 tablespoons flour
Edible flowers (such as nasturtium) or
    herb sprigs for garnish (optional)

In a small saucepan, combine the dried figs, shallots, veal stock, Madeira, and 3 tablespoons of the port. Bring to a boil. Reduce heat and simmer slowly until the liquid is thick and syrupy, about 8 to 10 minutes.

Transfer the mixture to a blender, add 2 tablespoons of the butter and the chicken stock, and purée until smooth. Pass the sauce through a fine mesh strainer and finish with part or all of the remaining port, depending on the sweetness the figs have given the sauce.

Lightly toast the pistachio nuts on a baking sheet in a 325°F oven. Set aside to cool, then separate into halves.

Cut the fresh figs lengthwise into quarters if they are small, into 6 pieces if they are larger. Melt the remaining 2 tablespoons of butter over moderate heat in a medium-sized saucepan. Sauté the figs just until they are warm (do not allow them to cook until they have become soft), remove them from the saucepan and keep warm.

Wash the pan and set it over moderately high heat. Dredge the slices of *foie gras* in flour, shaking off any excess. Season them with salt and pepper. When the pan is hot, but not smoking, add the *foie gras* to the dry pan and cook until the slices are a deep golden color on both sides, turning them once. They should feel soft, but not flabby, when pressed with a finger.

Arrange the slices of *foie gras* on four appetizer plates and nap with the sauce. Fan the slices of fresh fig out around the *foie gras*, and sprinkle with the pistachio nuts. Garnish with the flowers or herbs.

GERRI GILLILAND
Gilliland's · Santa Monica

"Being Irish, and coming to America ten years ago as a rather broke kid and today owning my own restaurant . . . you can't beat it, can you? In Ireland, the odds of something like that happening to a young woman are so, so small. America has been very good to me.

"Being a chef enabled me to carve out quite a life for myself. I am really thankful that my mother wasn't a cook, and so I became one. My life with food has had many phases, from cooking for my family, to studying it in school, to catering in Ireland and then in America. All of that led me to becoming a restaurant owner and a chef.

"Nothing could really have prepared me for that role. To be good and succeed, you must either be driven or crazy—or both. From the day you embark seriously on such a career, your life will never be your own or the same. The rewards, however, are great. When strangers or friends have finished a meal and warmly thank you . . . it makes everything worthwhile."

Gerri Gilliland

BLARNEY CHEESE & ONION TART

A quiche-like tart.

PASTRY

1¼ cups unbleached, all-purpose flour
Pinch salt
6 tablespoons sweet butter
1 small egg yolk
¼ cup sour cream

Place the flour and salt in the bowl of a food processor. Add the butter and process until the mixture is crumbly. Add the egg yolk and sour cream. Process by turning on and off again, quickly, until the dough begins to mass together.

Dump it out onto a floured board and form the pastry into a large ball. Wrap in plastic and chill for 1 hour. Roll out the pastry, and line an 11-inch flan tin with it. Prick the dough well, line the pastry shell with foil, and chill for 5 minutes. To prevent it from becoming soggy, bake the unfilled shell at 425°F for 5 minutes.

FILLING

4 ounces Blarney cheese (Swedish Fontina or a good Swiss cheese that will melt easily may be substituted)
2 pounds onions
4 tablespoons sweet butter
1 cup heavy cream
3 large egg yolks
1 large egg
Salt and pepper
Nutmeg to taste (a quick grinding)

Grate the Blarney cheese in a food processor, using the metal blade. Remove and set aside.

Also in the food processor, slice the onions, using the medium slicing disc.

Melt the butter and cook the onions on low heat for about 45 minutes, until they are very soft and golden brown.

Mix the cream with the yolks and the whole egg. Season with salt and pepper, and a grating of nutmeg.

Scatter the onions over the partially baked pastry. Then scatter the grated Blarney cheese over the onions. Pour the egg mixture over the onions and cheese.

Bake at 325°F for 35 minutes until the quiche is puffed and golden.

LILLIAN HAINES
Chef & Catering Consultant · Beverly Hills

With spunk and enthusiastic dedication, Lillian Haines became the pioneer for women in the professional kitchen, the first woman in the United States to earn the title of Certified Executive Chef, from the American Academy of Chefs, and the first woman to be elected into that élite group.

Lillian Haines

Lillian's career began when she took on the jobs of cook, party-planner, and chief dish-and-bottle washer in the family business, the first catering company in Southern California, established in 1930 in Beverly Hills by her mother-in-law, Hanchen Haines. Both her husband, Bill, and mother-in-law, Hanchen, died in 1957, leaving Lillian to run the business.

Having decided to keep the business going, and being confident that she was already a first-class cook and party-planner, she spent her evenings taking all the necessary classes for executive training offered by the Graduate School of Business Administration at the University of California, in Los Angeles. One such course was "How to Keep Generations of Clients Coming Back." And what clients: She has prepared parties for Presidents Dwight D. Eisenhower,

Lyndon B. Johnson, and John F. Kennedy, as well as for numerous other leaders in politics, society, business, and the arts. She was part of the team that planned and prepared the food for the first two-man orbit into space.

She offers this advice to those entering the food business: "Experiment and be willing to do anything and make sure you like it. Just because cooking at home is fun doesn't mean you'll like the pressure of cooking professionally.

"Get all the experience you can. If a pinch on the derrière is going to injure your psyche permanently, you are setting up your own roadblocks.

"Opportunity is always there if you are willing to receive it. Even if you have to work for nothing, grab as much experience wherever and whenever you can. When you are willing to embrace the world, the world is willing to embrace you."

. . .

MERINGUE LORENZO LOTTO

SERVES EIGHT TO TEN

MERINGUE

8 egg whites (1 cup)
¼ teaspoon cream of tartar
⅛ teaspoon vanilla extract
¼ teaspoon salt
1 cup superfine sugar

FILLING

2 cups chilled whipping cream
½ cup sugar (if using dark chocolate, add 2 tablespoons more sugar)
½ cup toasted almonds, chopped
10 ounces milk or dark sweet chocolate bars, coarsely chopped

Preheat oven to 200°F, or its lowest setting.

Place the egg whites in a mixer and beat until frothy. Add the cream of tartar and continue beating until soft peaks form. Add the vanilla and salt. Gradually beat in the 1 cup of superfine sugar, 2 tablespoons at a time, and continue beating until the egg whites are glossy and very, very thick.

Line two baking sheets with parchment paper or grease and flour them. Shake off the excess flour. Trace two 7½-inch circles in the flour. (Make the circles 10 inches in diameter if the recipe is being doubled.)

Fill a pastry bag fitted with a star tip with the meringue and trace the perimeter of a circle with it. Continue piping in decreasing circles to the center and then complete the second circle. Pipe out the rest of the meringue onto the baking sheets at random: the shape does not matter since these pieces will be chopped up for garnish.

Bake until the circles are completely crisp and firm, about 2 hours. Perfect meringue is crisp and snow white. Remove from the oven and allow to cool thoroughly.

One or two days before serving, whip the cream and gradually beat in the sugar. Place one meringue circle on a serving dish, spread it lavishly with ⅓ of the whipped cream. Sprinkle with ½ of the nuts and chocolate and press them into the cream. Cover with the second meringue circle. With a spatula smooth over the top and sides with the remaining cream.

Chop the random pieces of meringue and use them to coat the sides of the cake. Garnish the top with the remaining chopped almonds and chocolate and press them into the whipped cream. Refrigerate or freeze.

MICHELE ANNA JORDAN
The Brass Ass Saloon & The Jaded Palate · Cotati

"I joined The Brass Ass just three years ago, long after it had established itself as a Sonoma County tradition. I was lucky to have a broad base of loyal customers already established, and it's been satisfying to watch their responses to the new directions I've taken the menu.

Michele Anna Jordan

"I'm in the restaurant business primarily because I love food and love feeding people. The satisfied sigh of a customer, the smile my food puts on someone's face, is always a thrill, and always provides a little spark of inspiration to see how else I can please these eager palates.

"As the working partner at The Brass Ass, I have the opportunity, as well as the obligation, of course, to be in touch with all aspects of the business. Developing new recipes and creating specials keeps my hands in food, where I prefer them to be much of the time. My overall involvement with the restaurant keeps me in continual contact with the customers, too, and the constant response I get to my food is one of the things that insures its vitality. I have a great deal of control over the customer's total experience, a responsibility I welcome.

"Sonoma County is a marvelous place to be in the food business. The area is so alive, with a wonderful panorama of talent, products, and eager consumers, ready to try new things, ready to explore our county's luscious bounty. A unique aspect of my situation here comes through the column that I write. Since it is about food and not restaurants, there is no conflict of interest when it comes to discussing the restaurant. I frequently try out new recipes at the restaurant or in my catering business, The Jaded Palate. My readers know this. They know they can come for lunch and try what they've read about or talk to me about the column. It's another great way to continue my on-going dialogue about food."

•   •   •

BLUEBERRY & CHICKEN LIVER SALAD WITH BLUEBERRY VINAIGRETTE

SERVES FOUR

½ cup plus 3 tablespoons olive oil
6 tablespoons blueberry vinegar
1½ teaspoons ground cloves
Salt
Freshly cracked black pepper
¾ pound chicken livers
1 large or 2 small bunches young spinach
3 shallots, minced
1 cup fresh blueberries
8 to 10 soft-boiled quails' eggs or 4 soft-boiled eggs

To the ½ cup olive oil, add 3 tablespoons blueberry vinegar, 1 teaspoon cloves, and salt and pepper to taste. Set aside.

Trim, rinse, and dry the livers. Set aside.

Rinse and dry the spinach and toss with a small amount of olive oil until each leaf is coated. Arrange on a serving platter or on individual serving plates.

Cut each liver into 4 pieces and toss with salt, pepper, and ½ teaspoon cloves. Sauté the minced shallots in 3 tablespoons olive oil until they are just transparent. Add the livers and sauté quickly, about 1½ minutes on each side. Remove the livers from the pan with a slotted spoon and place them in a mixing bowl.

Deglaze the pan with the remaining 3 tablespoons blueberry vinegar. Pour the liquid over the chicken livers and toss well. Arrange the warm livers on top of the spinach and drizzle with the warm pan drippings and juice from the livers combined.

Sprinkle the blueberries decoratively over the salad and garnish with the quails' eggs, each cut in half through the shell (don't attempt to shell them), arranged around the edge of the platter. If you are using regular eggs, shell them, cut them in half, and arrange them. Serve with the blueberry vinaigrette on the side.

DONNA KATZL

Café for All Seasons · San Francisco

"In the earlier days of my life, when I was in a state of depression and severe agoraphobia, I felt hopeless; I had to fight to stay alive.

"There was one area that was very spiritual for me and, when I was involved with it, I felt at peace—that was when I was cooking and working with food. I can say with honesty that my love for cooking and food kept me alive through those dark times.

"As the years went by, I recovered and now, in my late forties, with no formal training, I am chef of a San Francisco restaurant in which I am also part-owner.

"Through my relationship with food came a wonderful relationship with myself and an ever-expanding group of great people. Food still enriches my life today. I believe and have experienced that nothing need stand in one's way—including one-self—in finding what the world has to offer."

Donna Katzl

ORZO PASTA SALAD

SERVES SIX
TO EIGHT

DRESSING
³⁄₄ cup olive oil
¼ cup white wine vinegar
2 teaspoons fresh rosemary, finely chopped
3 cloves garlic, finely minced
1 teaspoon Dijon mustard
2 teaspoons soy sauce
1½ teaspoons each salt and pepper

SALAD
3 cups cooked orzo (rice-shaped pasta),
    or you may use rice instead
¼ cup (a small can) pimientos, drained
    and chopped
1 tablespoon chives, finely chopped
1½ cups cooked, boned chicken pieces
½ pound baby Bay shrimp (usually only
    obtainable canned)
1 small green pepper, roasted, skinned,
    seeded, and chopped
1 small can black olives, drained and
    sliced

GARNISH
4 eggs, hard-boiled
Watercress sprigs
Whole black olives

Mix together the ingredients for the dressing and set aside.

In another bowl, mix together the ingredients for the salad, add the dressing, and toss until well combined. Adjust seasoning to taste.

Refrigerate for 2 hours to marinate.

Garnish with the hard-boiled eggs cut into halves, watercress sprigs, and whole black olives.

HEIDI KRAHLING
Butler's & Perry's · Mill Valley

"I have come to think of myself in terms of today's culinary atmosphere not so much as a woman chef, but rather as a chef who is a woman. I do realize, however, that the route that I and other women have followed to become chefs might be somewhat different from that followed by a man.

"As a child, I always enjoyed being a part of the cooking and other festivities that surrounded a holiday, and think that I received a great deal of satisfaction from nurturing my family with the dishes that I helped to prepare. My satisfaction has carried over to this day and I find that most of my gratification comes from the satisfaction of my customers.

"Most of the cooks with whom I work are women, and I feel that most of them share this respect for the nurturing aspect of cooking. This profession has not until recently been the domain of a large number of women, and I feel that the power, fame, and prestige take a back seat for most of us. I, for one, am primarily interested in the effect that my creations have on those who might enjoy them.

"In my reading, I came upon an ancient and absurd proverb which

Heidi Krahling

reads, "Woman does not understand what food means, and yet she insists on being a cook." I understand very well what food means. For me, it is a means of expression and a means of giving comfort and joy to others. My experience is that a great many women have come to understand what food is about and how using and sharing this knowledge can benefit others. It is this nurturing aspect of food that has led many women into this profession."

139

CORN FRITTERS

SERVES FOUR TO SIX

This is a basic soft fritter dough to which cheese, spices, or vegetables other than corn may added by the cook.

1¼ cups flour
2¼ teaspoons baking powder
1 teaspoon salt
2 eggs, separated
1 cup buttermilk
1½ teaspoons vegetable oil
2 cups corn kernels
½ cup diced onions
1 or 2 red jalapeño *chilies, seeded, and finely diced*
¼ cup chopped cilantro
Vegetable oil for frying

Sift the dry ingredients together.

Beat the egg yolks, buttermilk, and oil together and gradually add the flour mixture.

Beat the egg whites until they are stiff and fold them into the batter.

Gently stir in the corn, diced onion, *jalapeños*, and cilantro.

Deep fry by the spoonful.

FAYE LEVY

Cookbook Writer & Cooking Teacher · Santa Monica

Faye Levy has been described by the food editor of *Gourmet* magazine as "one of the finest cooks in the country." Her recent book, *Chocolate Sensations*, has been called "the chocolate book to end them all" by the editor-in-chief of *Cook's* magazine. In her new series, *Fresh from France*, the first book, *Vegetable Creations*, was just published. Faye has been writing a column called The Basics for *Bon Appétit* magazine since 1982. Her creative dishes have been featured on the covers of *Bon Appétit* and *Gourmet*. Her articles have been published in other national magazines and in numerous major newspapers.

Born and brought up in Washington, D.C., Faye has lived in three continents and has written cookbooks in three languages. She has the distinction of being the first American to have been commissioned to write a book by Flammarion, among the most distinguished publishers in France. *La Cuisine du Poisson*, written with master chef Fernand Chambrette, was published in 1984. Three cookbooks Faye wrote in Hebrew were published by a leading Israeli publisher.

Faye holds the Grand Diplome of the first graduating class from La

Faye Levy

Varenne, the cooking school in Paris where she spent over five years. She wrote the school's first cookbook, *The La Varenne Tour Book*, and as La Varenne's editor, developed and drafted the recipes for the school's other cookbooks and planned its curriculum.

CHOCOLATE-FLECKED MACADAMIA NUT TORTE

SERVES TEN
TO TWELVE

The macadamia nuts add enough richness to this torte so that no butter is necessary. Because they are so rich, macadamia nuts cannot be pulverized to a flour-like consistency and should be ground just to very fine pieces.

CAKE

2⅓ *cups (about 10 ounces) raw*
   macadamia nuts
2 *ounces semisweet chocolate, cut into bits*
¾ *cup sugar*
¼ *cup all-purpose flour*
½ *teaspoon double-acting baking powder*
5 *large eggs, separated, at room*
   temperature
¼ *teaspoon cream of tartar*

CHOCOLATE CREAM

1 *ounce semisweet chocolate, cut into bits*
1½ *tablespoons macadamia nut liqueur or*
   Frangelico (hazelnut liqueur)
¾ *cup well-chilled whipping cream*
2 *teaspoons sugar*
2 *tablespoons macadamia nut liqueur or*
   Frangelico (for sprinkling)
10 *whole raw macadamia nuts for garnish*

For the cake: Preheat oven to 325°F. Butter a 9-inch round springform cake pan about 3 inches deep and line its base with parchment paper or foil,

shiny side down. Butter and flour the paper or foil and the sides of the pan.

In a food processor chop the chocolate fine and transfer it to a large bowl. Combine 1 cup of the nuts with 3 tablespoons of the sugar in food processor, grind the nuts as fine as possible, and transfer them to the bowl. Repeat with the remaining nuts and another 3 tablespoons of sugar. Sift in the flour and baking powder and stir the mixture with a fork until it is thoroughly blended. Separate any lumps by rubbing them gently between your fingers.

With an electric mixer beat the egg yolks with ¼ cup of sugar, in a large bowl for about 5 minutes, or until mixture forms ribbons when the beaters are lifted. With an electric mixer beat the egg whites in another large bowl at moderate speed until they are frothy, add the cream of tartar, and continue to beat whites until they hold soft peaks. Gradually beat in the remaining 2 tablespoons sugar at high speed and then beat the whites until they are stiff. Sprinkle ⅓ of the nut mixture over the egg yolks and fold it in gently. Spoon ⅓ of the whites on top and fold them in gently. Repeat until all of the nut mixture and the egg whites are added. Continue folding only until batter is blended and no white streaks remain.

Pour batter into the prepared pan, quickly spread it as evenly as possible, and bake it in middle of the oven for about 55 minutes, or until a tester comes out clean. Let the cake cool in the pan on a rack for 10 minutes. Run a metal spatula or thin-bladed flexible knife around the sides of the cake, turn it out onto a rack, and remove the sides and base of the pan. Carefully peel off the paper. Let the cake cool completely. (The cake keeps, wrapped tightly in plastic wrap, for up to 2 days at room temperature; or it can be frozen.)

For the chocolate nut cream: Melt the chocolate in a double boiler over low heat. Stir the chocolate until it is smooth, add the liqueur, and remove mixture from heat, leaving it over the hot water. In a chilled bowl beat the cream with the sugar until it holds stiff peaks. Remove the chocolate from the double boiler and let it cool for half a minute. Quickly stir about ⅓ cup of whipped cream into the chocolate mixture. Quickly fold the chocolate mixture into the remaining whipped cream.

Using a pastry brush and holding it flat, dab the top and sides of the cake evenly with liqueur. Spread the chocolate cream on sides and top of cake. Garnish the top of the cake with whole macadamia nuts. Chill for 1 hour before serving. (The frosted cake keeps, covered when the the frosting is firm, for up to 1 day in the refrigerator.)

NOTE

If raw macadamia nuts are not available, use lightly salted nuts and desalt them. Put the nuts in a large strainer and rinse them with warm water for about 10 seconds, tossing them often. Drain them for 5 minutes in the strainer, tossing them occasionally. Transfer them to a baking sheet and dry in a preheated 250°F oven for 5 minutes, shaking the baking sheet occasionally. Transfer them to a plate and let them cool completely. Set aside 10 nuts for garnish and proceed with the recipe.

MICAELA LIVINGSTON
Ports · Los Angeles

Micaela Livingston

"Food is an irrational pleasure. Once cooking begins, it's all momentum. I became involved in the restaurant business because my husband wanted me to, but I already had an inherent respect for the process of cooking and taking care of people. We opened our first restaurant, the Studio Grill, in 1970. It was three blocks from our house. We had a professional stove in our kitchen at home, and I would cook there and run down the alley carrying food to the waiting customers. My husband, Jock Livingston, wore a doctor's lab coat while working in the restaurant. He looked a lot like Orson Welles. There's nothing like having a large person for a host. Imagine being greeted at the door by a 300-lb. man, who looked primitive and sensual at the same time. Jock was a symbol of satisfaction. From the start, we were fashionably underground, and we were lucky that our customers got it right away. We called it anonymous cooking.

"Billy Wilder, the director, was one of our first customers. Our restaurant was amusing as well to Jack Lemmon and Walter Matthau. One night, when they were there, I threw a brandy cream pie at our partner in reaction to his male chauvinism. Now, years later, I wonder how many other women in my business have ever felt like doing the same thing.

"In 1972, we opened Ports a little further east on the Santa Monica Boulevard strip. It was, at the time, a bar called the Sports Inn. Because we couldn't afford to have a new sign made, we simply painted over the S and the second word; thus, we created a new name for the restaurant. There was a pool table where our dining room is now, and a television set behind the bar. I suppose I had read too many Victorian novels, because what I really wanted to do was serve tea for the gentry—lemon curd or ham chutney sandwiches, that sort of thing. I even bought a couch from the set of my favorite movie but it never fit in with the decor.

"Ports allowed me to become the misfit chef that I always suspected I was. Soon, I was preparing *paella* and steak and kidney pie. *Empanadas* were a favorite. Perhaps the best example of my cross-cultural breeding (without over-refinement, thank you!) is in the sweetbreads with black mushrooms in oyster sauce. Together, Jock and I devised ways to prepare food that would be just as appropriate served in this century as in the ones gone by.

"I believe that Ports has contributed in a mischievous way to the food sensibility of Los Angeles. Our cooking has never been polite, but it's always had a certain grandeur about it. We created a personal world for ourselves in our restaurants and I hope that this world has touched the lives of our customers in some way. Since 1970 I've baked nearly twenty-five hundred brandy cream pies, one at a time. The best part is that none of them has tasted the same."

SWEETBREADS IN OYSTER SAUCE WITH CHINESE MUSHROOMS

SERVES FOUR, OR TWO AS A MAIN COURSE

1 pound sweetbreads
1 cup dried Chinese black mushrooms
1 onion, minced finely
1 clove garlic, minced
2 teaspoons fresh ginger, minced finely

SAUCE
1 teaspoon sugar
1 tablespoon soy sauce
4 tablespoons oyster sauce
3 tablespoons dry sherry or sake
2 tablespoons cornstarch
½ cup chicken stock

GARNISH
Scallions, finely chopped

Prepare the sweetbreads by soaking them in cold salted water for several hours. Clean off as much membrane as can easily be removed. Simmer the sweetbreads, together with a few lemon slices, in water, or in a *court bouillon* if desired, for about 12 minutes.

Put the sweetbreads into cold water and clean again, removing as much membrane as possible. Place a weight on top of the sweetbreads and refrigerate until ready to use—this makes them easier to slice. When you

MICAELA LIVINGSTON · 145

are ready to cook them, trim them
and cut them, on the diagonal, into
½-inch slices.

Soak the dried mushrooms in warm
water for 30 minutes. Drain them,
squeeze out the excess moisture,
remove and discard the stems, cut the
mushrooms into pieces, and reserve.

Sauté the onion, garlic, and ginger
until soft. Add the sliced sweetbreads
and the mushroom pieces. Mix and
leave over a low heat while preparing
the sauce.

Combine the sugar, soy sauce, oyster sauce, and sherry or *sake*, and use
this mixture to coat the sweetbreads.

Heat the chicken stock and dissolve the cornstarch in it. Strain to
remove any lumps and add to the
sweetbread mixture.

Stir the sweetbreads over a low
heat until the sauce has thickened and
is perfectly clear. Sprinkle the scallions on top, as a garnish.

DANG MANOPHINIVES
The Siamese Garden & Rosalynn Thai Restaurant · Venice

Dang Manophinives grew up in Bangkok, Thailand, the youngest daughter of a successful businessman and a woman who loved to cook. In Thailand women chefs are the tradition instead of the exception. Dang's mother, Suree Buranasombati, developed a cottage industry. She created ices, known as *van yen*, and other desserts and sold them to restaurants and caterers. Dang's sister, Apipat, went on to establish a restaurant called Suvalak in Bangkok in 1972. The food business runs in the family.

Dang came to this country in 1970 to study business at Campton College. At night she worked as a waitress at her cousin's Tepparod Tea House, one of the first Thai restaurants to become well known in Los Angeles. Soon Dang became a partner in the restaurant.

In 1978 Dang and her husband, Ban, opened the Siamese Garden on the edge of Venice and Marina del Rey. They transformed a funky, beachside sandwich shop into an intimate, elegant restaurant. The booths are lined with brocade and can be curtained off for privacy. The other tables are small and always decorated

Dang Manophinives

with roses arranged in elaborately stamped tin vases from Thailand.

In 1984 the two of them opened a second restaurant, Rosalynn, which they named after their daughter. Here the interior is strikingly postmodern, with its deep maroons offset by grays and silvers.

To watch Dang work in the kitchen today is to watch an experienced chef. The stainless steel stove glistens beside a shelf neatly stacked with square containers of her staples, chilies, spices, oils. She measures the ingredients by eye and then tastes at each step. Every dish is separately prepared to order, so diners must relax and converse while they wait. Although Dang has a *sous chef*, she does all the cooking herself, using frying pans instead of woks because she feels they are easier to handle.

Each dish is finished with delicately cut radish roses, carrot ribbons, and red cabbage curlicues. (Plate ornamentation is such an integral part of the Thai culinary art that the local Los Angeles temple offers Sunday classes in vegetable carving.)

The success of the Siamese Garden and Rosalynn are proper blessings from Mae Nang Kuak, the goddess who brings good luck and who has presided over Dang's first restaurant since it opened.

HOT & SOUR SHRIMP SOUP

SERVES TWO

2½ *cups chicken broth*
1 *tablespoon lemon grass, chopped*
   (include the big stalks for their smell)
2 *tablespoons fish sauce (available from*
   Asian grocers)
4 *straw mushrooms*
⅛ *teaspoon sugar*
½ *teaspoon* serrano *chilies, finely*
   chopped
8 *medium shrimp*
2 *tablespoons lime juice*
¼ *cup cilantro leaves*

To the chicken broth, add the lemon grass, fish sauce, mushrooms, sugar, and chilies. Cook at a high simmer for between 5 and 7 minutes.

Add the shrimp and bring the soup back to the boil. Turn off the heat and add the lime juice, which will cause the soup to cloud. Remove the lemon grass and add more lime juice to taste.

Garnish with cilantro leaves.

NOTE
The recipe may be doubled to serve as a first course for between 4 and 6 people.

KRISTIN MATHISON &
CAROL MICKELSEN
San Benito House · *Half Moon Bay*

"Cooking today is so alive, especially in California, where we have the freshest ingredients at our fingertips. Cooking schools and classes abound in the Bay Area, offering beginners and professionals the opportunity to pursue their food interests.

"The best advice I could give a novice cook is this: Learn how to make a veal stock, a chicken stock, a fish fumet; how to deglaze and when to add cream; know how to sharpen a knife; how to cut a piece of meat or poultry; and, above all . . . *TASTE!* Armed with the confidence knowing the basics brings, you will find that the rest all falls into place."

Kristin Mathison

"My start as a professional chef began with a card table and a cigar box. My husband, Ron, owns a nursery and consequently works weekends. As a school teacher, I was left with spare time on the Saturdays and Sundays that he was away; I needed something to do. I had learned to make hand-stretched dough and we had several apple trees . . . so, I

Carol Mickelsen and Kristin Mathison

decided to try my luck at selling apple strudel at the nursery.

"Early in the morning, I would stretch the dough, cut up the apples, and concoct my strudel. I spread a lace cloth over a card table, put out portions of strudel, plugged in the coffee pot, and left a cigar box for people to pay me on the honor system.

"The first day I came back to check the box, my heart was fluttering. I saw that a lot of strudel was gone, but had the customers paid? I opened the box to a thrill of dollar bills. The money matched up exactly to the amount of strudel and coffee that had been taken. I was hooked on

149

making munchies for public consumption.

"After the summer, I decided to tackle a larger project. The laundromat I owned had some empty rooms in back. Searching through restaurant supply catalogues, I found a stove and sink, dishes, pots, and pans. My husband and I decorated one room, and created a romantic, very small dining room. My friends always had loved to come to the house for dinner . . . but would they come to my little restaurant and pay?

"I sent out postcards with the menu and called it, 'Friends for Dinner.' The evening was prepaid by check. They loved it! The second seating would hang around the kitchen, while the first seating was finishing up. I cooked and my husband waited tables. We washed the dishes together.

"This concept of having friends for dinner is one I still try to maintain at San Benito House. Customers still come by the kitchen and chat . . . we love it!"

Carol Mickelsen

HALF MOON BAY SWEET PUMPKIN RAVIOLI

SERVES FOUR TO SIX

We tried for years to make ravioli successfully in large quantities. It wasn't until we started using the Ravioli Form, a simple frame made by Berarducci Brothers and costing about $7.00 in kitchen equipment stores, that we finally managed. Since then, however, we have reverted to making ravioli without the frame. Be sure to use the small, sweet pumpkins, not the jack-o'-lantern pumpkins for this dish.

SWEET PUMPKIN FILLING
1 pound sweet pumpkin or winter squash
1½ tablespoons butter
½ cup chopped leeks
1 teaspoon pressed garlic (optional)
2 teaspoons nutmeg
Salt and pepper
2 to 3 tablespoons cream

Clean the pumpkin of its seeds, cut into large chunks and then steam over water until the pulp is very soft. In the butter, sauté the leeks until they are soft and transparent, add the garlic and cook for 1 minute more. Scoop out the cooked pumpkin or squash pulp and process it, in small batches, with the leeks, in a food processor. Add the nutmeg, salt and pepper to taste, and enough cream to process the mixture. Keep the filling on the dry side, but it must be very smooth.

Cool to room temperature.

PASTA DOUGH
1½ cups all-purpose flour
1½ cups semolina flour
3 eggs
2 teaspoons salt
1 tablespoon water

Mix the two flours together and, on a work surface, mound them up, making a well in the center.

Beat the eggs lightly with the salt and the water and pour this mixture into the well.

Using a fork, slowly incorporate the egg mixture into the flour, working from the inner rim of the well. Work so that the egg and flour mixture is always smooth and do not try to incorporate too much flour at once, or you will have lumps. When the mixture gets too heavy for a fork, push the remaining flour to one side and, using a scraper, gently knead the dough, incorporating more flour gradually, until you finally have a smooth elastic ball.

Wrap the dough in plastic and let it rest, at room temperature for 1 hour.

When the dough has rested, divide the ball into 4 parts. Using a pasta machine, stretch the pasta to the machine's thinnest setting, all the while trying to keep the ribbon of dough the same width as the ravioli form.

Carefully lay a sheet of pasta over the ravioli form, if you are using one, and place 1 teaspoon of pumpkin filling into each ravioli space. Lay another sheet of pasta over the filling and seal the ravioli with a rolling pin pushed firmly over the top. If you are not using a ravioli form, simply lay 1 sheet of pasta on your work surface, dot it with teaspoonfuls of filling placed in rows about 1 inch (or the width of two fingers) apart, lay a second sheet on top, and cut through both layers with a crimped wheel.

Turn the ravioli over, onto a semolina-dusted tray, let them dry a bit, uncovered, in the refrigerator and then, covering them with parchment paper or a tea towel, leave them in the refrigerator until you are ready to cook them.

To cook, bring a large saucepan of cold water to the boil. Add enough salt so that the water actually tastes salty. Add the pasta and cook at a gentle boil until the ravioli are done, about 2 to 4 minutes. Gently lift out the pasta with a slotted spoon and place in a dish containing the warmed cream sauce.

Sprinkle with Parmesan cheese and serve immediately, garnished with whatever herb was used in the sauce (*recipe follows*).

SAUCE

2 cups whipping cream
Fresh herbs, such as parsley, basil, thyme,
oregano, chervil, or marjoram, finely
chopped or cut into a chiffonnade
Garlic
Salt and pepper

Warm the cream just until it is heated
through, add the herbs, garlic, and
salt and pepper to taste and pour into
a warmed serving dish ready to take
the ravioli as soon as they are cooked.

ALICE MEDRICH
Cocolat · Berkeley

Alice Medrich is the founder and owner of Cocolat and the person who introduced the chocolate truffle to America. Her pastry and dessert making is largely self-taught. She has always had an interest in food, and was especially enthralled by chocolate. "I was raised on Hershey bars. I adore chocolate."

In 1972, when Alice and her husband, Elliott, were living in Paris for a year, she discovered the world of French desserts and fell in love with chocolate truffles, confections which were to become the trademark of Cocolat. "Truffles were so different from American candy."

"I received much guidance and inspiration from people not necessarily famous, but masters of their craft nonetheless. I'll be forever grateful to Suzanne Bergeaud, for instance. From her I learned the recipe for my first chocolate torte, the foundation for all of my chocolate cakes."

Upon returning to Berkeley, California, Alice began selling homemade truffles to various food shops in the Bay Area. "I did not have a great deal of formal training in France, so it was during the following two years [1973 and 1974] that I began to teach

Alice Medrich

myself the art of cooking, baking, and decorating with chocolate. I baked nearly every night, exploring both the repertoire of the professional *pâtissier* and the notebooks and cookbooks dear to the French housewife."

She also went back to France for private instruction with Camille Cadier, a cooking instructor and Simone Beck's assistant, and Marguerite La Pierre, a candymaker. She took courses at the Le Nôtre School outside Paris from Gaston Le Nôtre, and at a bakery in Reims, east of Paris, under the direction of chef Désire Valentine, Camille Cadier's brother-in-law.

Culinary influences back home included Simone Beck, Paula Peck, and Julia Child, whose recipes and methods Alice learned in her own kitchen. When she wasn't cooking, Alice was completing course work toward a Masters in Business Administration at the University of California, Berkeley.

Realizing that she preferred experimenting with truffles and making chocolate desserts, she stopped writing her MBA thesis and opened her first Cocolat shop in Berkeley shortly before Christmas, 1976. That day she sold out her inventory in three hours. Since then, six more stores have opened in the San Francisco Bay Area.

Looking back, she recalls a certain naïveté about running a business. She had hoped originally that, when customers "dropped by," she could brush the flour from her hands, wait on them, and then return to her baking. With Cocolat's growth she has chosen to leave the everyday details of running the business to others so that she can concentrate on creating desserts. A punctilious attention to quality has earned Alice an enviable reputation. According to the magazine, *Bon Appétit*, "The elegant sim-

plicity of her cakes and her devotion to pure ingredients have become trademarks."

Of her success Alice says, "I think of desserts as an art form—a chance to delight the eye and the mind as well as the palate. I believe in doing things the right way. We don't cut corners and, after ten years, we're still maniacs about good ingredients."

• • •

CHOCOLATE PECAN TORTE

SERVES EIGHT TO TEN

6 ounces semisweet or bittersweet baking chocolate
6 ounces sweet butter
4 large eggs
⅛ teaspoon cream of tartar
A pinch of salt
½ cup sugar
1 cup ground pecans
2 tablespoons sifted flour
¼ cup sugar

Preheat oven to 350°F. Grease and flour or line the bottom of a 9 inch by 2 inch round cake pan with parchment paper.

Melt the chocolate and butter in a small saucepan placed in a water bath on low heat. Stir occasionally until melted and smooth, then remove from heat. Meanwhile separate the eggs, placing the whites in a clean dry mixer bowl with the salt and cream of tartar. In another bowl whisk the yolks with ½ cup sugar until they are pale and form a ribbon when the beaters are lifted. Stir in the warm chocolate mixture, the nuts, and flour, and set the mixture aside.

Begin beating the reserved egg whites, salt, and cream of tartar at high speed. When soft peaks form, start sprinkling in the remaining ¼ cup sugar. Continue to beat until the egg whites are stiff but not dry. Fold about ⅓ of the meringue completely into the chocolate batter to lighten it, then quickly fold in the remaining meringue. Turn the mixture into the prepared pan and bake for 40 to 45 minutes. A toothpick plunged into the center of the cake should show moist crumbs—not dry, but not too runny. Cool the cake in the pan. Finish with Chocolate Glaze.

CHOCOLATE GLAZE

Use this glaze for desserts that are kept and served at room temperature. Properly handled, it will remain dark and shiny.

4 ounces sweet butter, cut into bits
6 ounces semisweet or bittersweet baking chocolate, cut into bits
5 tablespoons light corn syrup

Place the butter, chocolate, and corn syrup in a small saucepan and warm gently in a water bath over low heat. Stir frequently until the glaze is smooth and completely melted. Do not allow it to get too hot. Remove from heat and set it aside until nearly set. Use the refrigerator if you are in a hurry.

TO GLAZE THE CAKE

Allow the glaze to cool until it is almost set but still spreadable.

Run a knife around the edges of the completely cooled cake to release it from the sides of the pan. The cake will have settled in the center, leaving a high rim around the edges. Press this rim down firmly with your fingers so that it is level with the center of the cake. Now reverse the cake onto a cardboard circle cut exactly to fit. Peel away the parchment paper if you have used it. The bottom of the cake has now become the top.

Spread the sides and top of the cake with just enough cooled glaze to smooth out any imperfections, cracks, or ragged places. (This is the "crumb coat"—or preparation for final glazing.)

Very gently reheat the remaining glaze in a water bath just until it is smooth and pourable and the consistency of very heavy cream. It should be barely lukewarm. Strain the glaze through a very fine strainer to remove air bubbles or crumbs. Pour all of the glaze onto the center of the top of the cake. Use a clean dry metal spatula to coax the glaze over the edges of the cake, coating all the sides. Use as few strokes as possible. When the cake is completely coated, lift it off the plate and let it dry on a rack before moving it to its final serving platter.

The cake may be presented simply as it is or decorated: Press chopped or shaved toasted nuts around the sides of the cake just before the glaze hardens, or pipe melted chocolate through a paper cone for a more professional decoration.

MARY ETTA MOOSE
Washington Square Bar & Grill · San Francisco

"The career chef's best friend is her notebook. Significant observations, lessons taken from successes and failures, ideas and creations . . . the matters that form one's personal wisdom are swimming among the day's minutiae and should be plucked out and recorded before they escape. To lose such hard-gleaned information is wasteful.

"My notebooks are my vaults; I carry my current workbook about like an artist carries her sketchbook. Each page is numbered and headed by subject matter, so it can easily be indexed (e.g., Fish Butchering Techniques, Meat Ordering Specs, Aromatics for Sauces, etcetera). In the front of the book, I set up a 'page number/subject' index for easy retrieval and evaluation of the entries.

"One day, the successful chef will be asked to publish . . . and how thankful she will be for her notebooks then!"

Mary Etta Moose

RIGATONI LECSO

TUBE MACARONI WITH PEPPERS, TOMATO & ANDOUILLE SAUSAGE

SERVES SIX TO EIGHT

I developed this sauce for the corno di toros *peppers, which are available in the Bay Area for a couple of months, in August and September. They are thicker and sweeter than bell peppers, but bell peppers work very well.*

1½ pounds andouille *sausage or other smoked, hot link sausage, cut into ¼-inch dice*
1 tablespoon olive oil
2½ cups thinly sliced Spanish (yellow) onion
1 pound each long yellow and red corno di toros *sweet peppers, seeded and sliced into thin rounds*
2 pounds ripe summer tomatoes, peeled and diced
1 teaspoon sugar
2 level teaspoons kosher salt
1¾ tablespoons sweet Hungarian paprika.

Slowly heat a large, shallow, wide, heavy pan. Add the olive oil and heat it through. Add the sausage and allow it to cook gently without becoming crisp. When it has rendered enough fat to cook them, add the onions, keeping the heat very low.

After about 5 minutes, add the peppers to the onions. Cover the pan with a sheet of waxed paper and then its lid and cook for another 15 minutes.

Add the diced tomato, sugar, kosher salt, and paprika. Keeping the heat very low all the while, cook for another 15 to 20 minutes, until the sauce is thick.

Taste the sauce, adjust the seasonings, and toss with hot, drained pasta.

CATHERINE PANTSIOS
Zola's · San Francisco

"After working as a cook for twelve years, I'm coming to understand why French cooks call the stove *le piano*. It is, in fact, an instrument for the execution of our art, and yet it is rarely credited or approached with the respect it merits. It is easy to forget that we, as cooks, do not actually 'cook' at all. We mediate between the stove and the raw materials, allowing the heat produced by the stove, through control of its intensity, quality, and duration, to transform the raw ingredients and bring out their natural qualities. So, as with any craft, we learn through our daily work to understand and use the tools, materials, and procedures of our *métier*.

"The precision of modern equipment is reassuringly predictable. While the heat produced by wood or charcoal fires offers a range of qualities it can impart to food, it requires intelligent observation and an awareness of how the heat changes over time. Even a gas burner has an infinite number of notes in its scale, and its effect on food is further modified by the type of pan we use, if we choose to use the flame directly to scorch or roast, or if we alter the nature of the

Catherine Pantsios

heat by passing it through water or stock.

"Stove work is endlessly fascinating, whether simple scale-like exercises or more complex orchestrations of procedures. One comes to know one's stove and how to work with its different qualities in the realization of ideas. Sometimes, the limitations of our equipment, such as fewer burners or lack of a grill or salamander, force us to work in more depth with one

159

particular process, such as braising or slow cooking. The result is that we discover possibilities inherent in a technique that might not have been so fully explored, given a wider range of 'instrumentation.' Often, the most limited situations, in terms of equipment, turn out to be the most challenging and ultimately rewarding, by teaching us how we can do with so little. This give and take, this collaboration between the cook and her stove, makes for a very special relationship. Thus, at the end of the night, when I break down and scour the stove, it is with a tenderness and humility that I hope can somehow express to this not-so-inanimate object the respect I feel for it."

GARLIC SOUP

SERVES EIGHT

1 quart peeled garlic cloves
1 large onion
4 tablespoons extra virgin olive oil
4 tablespoons flour
1 quart chicken stock
2 cups heavy cream
3 egg yolks
½ cup grated Parmesan cheese

Sauté the garlic and onion in the olive oil until the onion is soft, but not brown. Sprinkle with flour and cook for another minute or two, stirring often. Add the stock and simmer until the garlic is meltingly soft. Purée in a blender or food mill.

Whisk together the cream and egg yolks. Slowly whisk in the hot soup. Reheat carefully; do not allow the soup to boil.

Serve with croutons and grated Parmesan cheese.

JUDY PROKUPEK
Manka's · Inverness

"My business is a family one, and my involvement with it began on August 19, 1962, my wedding day. I married into a 'restaurant family' and soon discovered that I had better learn to like cooking, as food and its preparation were always topics of discussion. I was apprenticed, so to speak, to my late husband, who, in turn, had been taught by his mother, an accomplished chef, schooled in her native Czechoslovakia. She and her family escaped after the Soviet takeover in 1948, emigrating first to Holland, then to Victoria, B.C., and, lastly, to Inverness, in California, where she still provides guests with her Czech pastries. Today, here at Manka's, all the basic food preparation falls into my hands, although I am skillfully aided by my two sons, aged nineteen and twenty-one. When they were very, very young, our kitchen was their playground and our sinks their playpens, with utensils, pots, and pans serving as their toys. They literally grew up in the business.

"I mention all this as I feel it is important, perhaps essential, to the vitality and creativity of this profession, to allow and encourage entry into it from directions other than

© Art Rogers/Point Reyes

Judy Prokupek

graduation from culinary institutes or professional cooking schools. Experience and the desire to create satisfying foods are invaluable assets."

161

OYSTERS BAKED ON THE HALF SHELL

SERVES FOUR

On the West Coast, Willapa Bay, Blue Point, and Belon oysters are freely available. Ths recipe is unlikely to be successful with canned or bottled oysters.

1 pound butter, softened
12 anchovy fillets, finely chopped
2 egg yolks
1 whole egg
4 cloves garlic, finely minced
2 tablespoons chopped fresh parsley
1 small onion, diced
2 tablespoons dried tarragon, or 3 tablespoons fresh tarragon leaves
⅓ cup dry white wine
¼ to ½ cup bread crumbs, to bind the mixture
⅛ teaspoon black pepper—and no salt

40 fresh oysters

Place all of the ingredients, except the oysters, in a bowl and mix thoroughly. Set aside.

Clean the oysters under cold running water. Open them carefully, with an oyster knife, taking pains not to spill any of the juices. Lay the oysters in their half shells in a shallow baking pan that has been lined with rock salt—the bed of salt keeps the shells from tipping over.

Cover each oyster with a spoonful of the anchovy-herb butter. Bake the oysters in a 400°F oven for 15 minutes, until the edges begin to curl slightly. Remove and sprinkle lightly with bread crumbs. Return to the oven to brown the bread crumbs lightly.

Serve in the shells, garnished with lemon wedges and parsley sprigs.

MARY RISLEY
Tante Marie's Cooking School · San Francisco

"Eating and cooking have been loves of mine ever since I can remember. In 1970 I decided I wanted to become an authority on food, so I systematically went about learning all I could. This included cooking courses here in San Francisco, at the London Cordon Bleu, and lots of reading and eating. In March 1973, I announced that I was going to give participation cooking classes in my home. Very quickly I was giving lots of demonstrations in stores such as Design Research and Williams-Sonoma and was a regular cook on a local morning television show.

"After five years of this, I made another career decision. Since I was beginning to get inquiries about courses that were more serious than those offered once a week and I was having to tell people that, for a real culinary education, they would have to go to Paris or London, I decided to open a full-time cooking school in San Francisco. Look at all the wonderful ingredients we have here and the great chefs. Using my background in investments, I raised some capital and formed a limited partnership to start a full-time cooking school. The school that I built

Mary Risley

opened in April, 1979. My concept was that I would teach the morning participation classes and have well-known Bay Area chefs and teachers give the afternoon demonstrations. That summer I had only one full-time student. What a lucky fellow he was—some of his teachers were Carlo Middione, Ken Hom, and Jeremiah Tower.

"Every quarter I published a schedule of classes so others could join the full-time students for the morning or afternoon classes. I continued to teach my evening classes three times a week. I never worked so hard in my life. My love for cooking became a devotion to teaching. Now, eight years later, I have a fully operating cooking school with morning, afternoon, and evening classes six days a week. Although the purpose of the school is to train professionals, we have classes for people at all levels of ability and interest.

"What I have seen in this area over the years is a genuine increase in knowledge and interest in food. In the early days, people wanted to learn to cook dishes that would impress their friends, dishes such as Beef Wellington and Grand Marnier Soufflé. Now, students want to learn theory and techniques that will give them a better understanding of food and better skills for creating simple and delicious meals to share with their friends. Fewer people are coming to classes for recreation; more are coming because they want to be professional cooks. After fifteen years, I consider myself very fortunate to be a part of a growing awareness of food and cooking, and, I still love it."

SAUTÉED CAMEMBERT

SERVES FOUR

1 Camembert cheese
1 egg, beaten
1 cup bread crumbs
3 tablespoons butter
1 tablespoon oil
¼ cup chopped chives

Dip the round of Camembert first into the beaten egg and then into bread crumbs.

In a heavy skillet melt 2 tablespoons of the butter with the oil. When this mixture is very hot, place the dipped and breaded Camembert into the skillet. After 2 or 3 minutes, when there is a nice brown crust on it, turn the cheese carefully with 2 metal spatulas, and brown the other side. Remove from the pan and keep warm.

Add to the pan the 1 remaining tablespoon of butter and the chives (the green part of scallions may be substituted) and cook these for a moment or two, then pour the mixture over the cheese. Garnish, if desired with a tomato rose, surround with water biscuits, and serve immediately.

VARIATION
Instead of the chives and the tomato rose, add ½ cup pine nuts to the last tablespoon of butter and sauté them gently before pouring the mixture over the warm cheese.

AMARYLL SCHWERTNER
Free-lance Chef · Oakland

"I came to cooking through my grandmother, a professional chef in Hungary and later in the U.S. My exposure to this role model, I feel, predisposed me to choose cooking as a vocation and a career. All the while she worked she would feed us three great meals a day. As a child I took this quite for granted; now as a mother, I use it as a constant reference.

"In 1979, coinciding with the birth of my child, opportunities within my work began to broaden and I had a chance to spend an extended time in Europe. I took the opportunity to start bringing my daughter with me to work both when possible and when necessary. I feel I gave her a resource of comfort through exposure that still enables her to visualize what I'm doing, the environment of the kitchen, and my emotional and pragmatic responses to my work. There are many times when complicated questions arise but I feel I have refined something and I am compelled to resolve the problems as they come up and to continue with what I have to do. As in all careers, and this applies to men and women, ideally one's work priorities are married (through an

Amaryll Schwertner

enormous amount of effort) to the whole of one's personal goals.

"My general recipe for all cooks is to suggest that they find the spirit of the food, not the formula. I feel that the most important component of a recipe is the quality of the ingredients and one's relationship to them. Recipes should not be regarded as static formulas but rather as an adjunct to the cook's palate, tools, ingredients, and interests. Frequently the simplest of ideas enhances or completely makes a dish memorable."

Simplicity—applied with a sense of
   fun and adventure
Coherent balance—of color, texture
   and the tastes of sweet, salt, and
   sour to complement one another
Skill or challenge—appropriate to
   one's time and tools

MUSHROOM RAGOUT

SERVES FOUR TO SIX

This dish can be served in a number of ways: as an appetizer, over garlic toasts; as a warm, first-course salad, with tiny spinach and arugula greens tossed in at the last minute; as a sauce over risotto *or* polenta; *or as a sauce for any roast or grilled meat or fish. Depending on how the ragout will be served, it may be finished in two different ways.*

½ *cup minced shallots*
4 *tablespoons sweet butter*
2 *pounds sliced mushrooms (assorted
   cèpes, chanterelles, field mushrooms,
   shiitake, etc., or any one of these
   varieties)*
½ *cup good quality red or white wine
   (Merlot for a savory, peppery, red wine
   sauce; Zinfandel for a sweeter sauce;
   any good dry white wine for a more
   distinctive mushroom flavor)*
½ *cup chicken or duck stock or* ½ *cup
   stock made from dried mushrooms*
Salt and coarsely ground white pepper
A squeeze of fresh lemon juice
Zest of half a lemon, minced finely

VARIATION ONE
4 *tablespoons cold sweet butter*
¼ *cup minced fresh herbs*
⅛ *cup heavy cream or* crème fraîche

VARIATION TWO
1 cup fresh tomatoes, diced
5 or 6 whole fresh sage leaves
2 tablespoons cold sweet butter

Sauté the shallots in 4 tablespoons of
sweet butter until they are transparent. Add the mushrooms and continue to sauté over a low heat until the
mushrooms have given off their liquid
into the butter.

Deglaze with the wine and reduce
the liquid by half. Add the stock, salt,
and pepper, and reduce by half again.
This entire cooking process will take
between 10 and 12 minutes. Then
spray in a few drops of lemon juice
and add the lemon zest.

For variation one, turn up the heat,
add the butter, herbs, and cream, and
reduce to a voluptuous but not thick
sauce.

For variation two, add the tomatoes, herbs, and butter, and cook over
medium heat. The butter will add
body to the ragout.

LYDIA SHIRE
The Four Seasons Hotel · Los Angeles

"It was the next logical step in my career to become the first woman executive chef in the country to open a deluxe hotel. I had headed the kitchens of Seasons, the popular restaurant in Boston's Bostonian Hotel, and it was hard to leave Boston, my hometown. But I have always felt chefs should move on if it means growing in the profession. The new Four Seasons Hotel in Los Angeles offered me my first chance to open a deluxe hotel.

"The excitement of California is the opportunity to work among so many young and creative chefs. Unlike the old days, I find today's chefs share their 'secrets,' and we all improve each other's work. Never have I felt discriminated against as a woman. Things are more open now, and dedication and hard work are the real criteria fine restaurants seek in chefs.

"Hotels differ from independent restaurants in that they require so many forms of food service: dining room meals, banquets, buffets, business and social functions, poolside snacks, room service and, what we call at the Four Seasons, alternative cuisine—a special lighter menu for

Lydia Shire

health-conscious guests. One plus is that we have lots of space for specialized kitchen equipment. Also, the resources of a hotel leave me free to buy any ingredients—things like a pound of truffles, that most regular restaurants could not indulge in. Still, I am able to operate the dining rooms as free-standing restaurants. In the days when every hotel had a food and beverage director, chefs had less freedom in designing menus and negotiat-

168

ing with purveyors. At the Four Seasons we have no food and beverage director. I am responsible for planning and ordering, but that also means I am free to be creative. The hotel has faith in me, and it gives me the backing to try new things.

"California cuisine usually implies simplicity in dishes. It's an unfussy food—a lot of grilling, a lot of salads. I mix a lot of other ethnic influences—Moroccan, Indian, Oriental—with the sense of balance I learned from classic French cooking. I create more involved dishes, which the average home cook could not do. They are complicated but, therefore, interesting.

"At the Four Seasons Hotel, I will change the menu each season to take advantage of each season's ingredients. You can buy asparagus year-round, but I like keeping it as a spring treat. We have an unusual menu of eleven main courses, nine appetizers, three soups, and two salads. Some of my first spring menus—for the hotel's opening—included Crisp Pastry of Braised Young Goat with Lemon, Dandelions and Warm Skordalia; Broiled Skate Ribs with Blossom Vinegar Sauce; and Caviar in a Chinese Lacquer Box, a main course consisting of eight or nine items such as *sashimi* of tuna, steamed smoked haddock, vegetable *tempura*, lacy potato cake and maybe an oyster.

"The secret to success in hotel kitchen work, I think, is to be very flexible. Unlike a restaurant, a hotel never shuts down. In deluxe hotels like the Four Seasons, there is often twenty-four-hour room service. And holidays for everyone else are major work days—and nights—for hotel chefs.

"I tell cooking students just to get their foot in the door. Take any position. There are always openings. Be willing to prove yourself. Aim for the best restaurants and stay until you have another quality position."

NOTE: Lydia has just announced, as we go to press, that she will be leaving the Four Seasons in order to open her own restaurant.

MOROCCAN PASTRY OF BLUEFISH & LOBSTER

SERVES FOUR

The Moroccan pastry called for in this recipe is known as warka *leaves, a recipe for which may be found in any Moroccan cookbook. According to Paula Wolfert, to make it is a labor of love. Phyllo or strudel dough may be substituted. (Forty* warka *leaves, each measuring about eight inches square are the equivalent of between half and three-quarters of a pound of phyllo dough.) The dish would probably taste similar; the spirit would have been changed—*warka *leaves and phyllo leaves are not synonymous. Similarly, bluefish may be replaced by any fish that flakes easily, for instance, halibut, but the dish will have been subtly altered thereby.*

2 lobsters, each weighing about 1¾
    pounds
2 pounds bluefish, scaled, boned, but not
    skinned
8 warka *leaves*

6 ripe tomatoes
½ cup mirepoix *(finely chopped carrot,
    onion, and celery)*
¼ cup plus 2 tablespoons olive oil
2 tablespoons cumin seeds
½ cup canned tomatoes, chopped
3 red peppers, roasted, peeled, seeded,
    and puréed
Salt and pepper

1 cup blanched almonds
5 cloves garlic
Juice of 1 lemon

Half a potato
A few pieces of bok choy
½ cup chopped cilantro

Slices of preserved lemon, for garnish

Cook the lobsters by blanching them for 8 minutes in boiling water. Cut the bluefish into ½-inch thick slices, leaving the skin on. Make the *warka* leaves according to the recipe.

To prepare the tomato *coulis*, blanch, peel, and coarsely chop the fresh tomatoes. Sauté the *mirepoix* in the ¼ cup of olive oil until the vegetables are soft. Add the tomatoes, 1 tablespoon of the cumin seeds, which have been crushed, and the ½ cup of chopped canned tomatoes. Simmer for 20 minutes and then strain the sauce. Add the red pepper purée and salt and pepper to taste.

To prepare the almond purée, toast the cup of almonds in a sauté pan, without using any oil, until they are golden. Then toast the remaining tablespoon of cumin seeds, in a tablespoon of olive oil over medium heat, until they are fragrant. Lightly sauté the garlic in the last remaining tablespoon of oil until the cloves are barely golden. Purée the almonds, cumin seeds, and garlic together in a blender, until the mixture is smooth. Add a little more olive oil if it is looking dry. Add the juice of 1 lemon.

Cut the peeled potato into ½-inch cubes, blanch until *al dente*, and cool. Stir fry the bok choy briefly in a little olive oil and minced garlic. Set the potato cubes aside, together with the bok choy, the chopped cilantro, and the preserved lemon slices.

To assemble the pastries, cut each *warka* leaf into the shape of a half moon. Place on it, in the center, a small piece of bok choy, a slice of bluefish, and about 2 ounces of lobster. Salt and pepper the fish and spoon some of the almond purée on it. Sprinkle over some of the potato cubes, cilantro, and lemon juice. Roll the half moon of pastry into a cone, completely enclosing the filling. When all the cones have been assembled—allow 2 per person for an entrée—sauté them slowly in olive oil, turning them once. Place them in a 350°F oven to finish cooking gently.

Serve on a dinner plate, with the tomato *coulis* alongside, and garnished with slices of preserved lemon and sprigs of cilantro.

DREW R. SPANGLER
Free-lance Chef · Mill Valley

Drew Spangler

"Recently the prejudice against women in the professional kitchen seems to have lessened, especially in the places that are doing California cuisine or the newer foods. Tips I would give other women interested in the business are the same as I give men—decide what interests you. What restaurant serves the kind of food you want to serve? Apply for a job there. Keep at it until you get the job. Don't settle for a position in a restaurant where you are not comfortable, or where you would not be proud to be serving the food."

CIOPPINO

SEAFOOD STEW

SERVES TEN

I originally served this dish at the Olema Inn's first Seafood Festival in May 1984. I wanted to do an authentic version and discovered, through research, that the origins of the dish are unclear. Numerous recipes exist, but the styles change radically from one recipe to the next. My solution was to draw on the common threads: tomatoes, onions, wine, herbs, and fish. The fish and shellfish used here are, or are similar to, varieties that are, or were, native to the San Francisco Bay and Tomales Bay.

FISH AND SHELLFISH
*1¼ pounds scallops
1½ pounds Tomales Bay mussels
1 pound Manila clams
20 rock crab claws
20 Monterey prawns
6 pounds whole Pacific rockfish*

Wash the scallops, removing any grit. Scrub the mussels and clams and de-beard them. Crack the crab claws. De-vein the prawns if you wish. Do leave the shells on if your guests will go for it. Fillet the fish, cut it into 1½-inch chunks, and reserve the bones for the *fumet*.

FUMET
1 large onion
2 carrots
1 stalk celery
3 sprigs fresh thyme
3 sprigs parsley
1 small bay leaf
Bones and trimmings of the fish, cleaned
    of blood and internal organs

Place all the ingredients into a pot. (Do not use an aluminum one.) Cover with cold water, bring to the boil, and skim the surface. Reduce to a simmer and cook for about 30 minutes. Remove from the heat and strain.

TOMATO BROTH
¾ pound onions
15 large garlic cloves (1¾ ounces),
    unpeeled
2 stalks celery (2 ounces)
3 tablespoons California virgin olive oil
4½ pounds ripe tomatoes
1½ cups red wine
1½ cups fumet

AROMATICS
2 small bay leaves
3 sprigs fresh oregano
¾ tablespoon fresh thyme
1 tablespoon fresh parsley
2½ tablespoons basil stalks
¾ tablespoon fresh summer savory
½ teaspoon cayenne pepper

Again, using a pot that is not made of aluminum, sauté the coarsely chopped onions, garlic, and celery in the olive oil until the onions are translucent. Core the tomatoes, cut into chunks, and add them to the pot with the wine and *fumet*. Cook over a low heat until the tomatoes are completely softened. Purée in a blender and strain the broth. Return the broth to the pot.

Add the aromatics and continue simmering for another 30 minutes. Strain again, and return to the stove.

Add the crab, clams, and mussels. Cover and cook for 2 minutes until the shellfish begin to open. Add the prawns, fish, and scallops. Cook until the fish is just done.

Portion out the fish and shellfish into bowls. Correct the seasoning of the broth and ladle it over the fish. Serve with crusty San Francisco sourdough bread.

BARBARA TROPP
China Moon Café · San Francisco

"People often, and rightly, speak of the positive side of women working together in a kitchen; the level of cooperation and caring for the food and one another is indeed remarkable.

"However, my own experience has impressed me, equally strongly, with a negative side of the same picture. Women working under the direction of a woman have an expectation and a deep psychological need of nurturing. This need often gets in the way of the work at hand. For example, the cook who repeatedly has been told to sharpen her knife skills in the preparation for a certain dish finally replies that her knife is dull. The chef, who if exercising a more typically 'male' response would tell her to pick up the honing steel nearby, instead picks up the steel and does the job herself as any caring mother might. It's a curious two-way street: the woman chef as mom and the woman cook as child.

"My own level of caring is so enormous, both about the quality of the food and the spirit that my cooks have in their work, that I function rather poorly if my contact with them is too close. For me, the middle-person of a kitchen manager (who, in our case, has always been a woman) is

Barbara Tropp

an essential distancing device. I can thus be the perfectionist I am without being the evil mother, and I can be the caring employer without being smothering or delivering the very mixed message: 'That carrot dice

174

looks lousy, but don't take it personally.'

"I sometimes think that if I had grown up in a large household or had children, I would be a lot better able to handle the dynamics of being a woman in charge. For me it is an emotional roller-coaster and is very likely to be the real meaning of doing this job, in that I'm learning something for my life, not just for my cuisine or my career."

HOT & SOUR SQUID

SERVES THREE OR FOUR

This is a gutsy dish with great contrasts of color, texture, and flavor. I love it best with a full-bodied Zinfandel and a hunk of crusty hot garlic bread or served on top of a pan-fried noodle pillow.

1 pound small squid, cleaned, tentacles reserved, and body cut crosswise into ½-inch rings

AROMATICS
1 tablespoon fresh ginger, very finely minced
1 tablespoon garlic, very finely minced
1 tablespoon Chinese salted black beans, unwashed
¼ teaspoon dried red chili flakes, or a mixture of thinly sliced rings of fresh red, green, and yellow chilies

LIQUIDS
½ cup rich chicken stock, unsalted
2½ tablespoons soy sauce
2 tablespoons Chinese rice wine or dry sherry
2½ tablespoons distilled white vinegar
¼ teaspoon sugar

(continued)

VEGETABLES

*½ pound trimmed carrots, cut on the
    diagonal into ⅛-inch coins*
*¾ pound slender zucchini, cut into ¼-
    inch rounds, or baby zucchini, cut
    lengthwise in half*
*1 cup red and yellow bell pepper squares
    3 to 4 tablespoons corn or peanut oil*
*1 tablespoon cornstarch dissolved in 1½
    tablespoons cold stock*

Combine the aromatics in a saucer
and the liquids in a bowl, stirring to
dissolve the sugar.

In a 1-quart saucepan, bring 2
cups of water to a slow simmer.

Heat a wok or large, heavy skillet
over high heat until it is hot enough
to evaporate a bead of water immediately. Reduce the heat to medium-
high, add the oil, and swirl to glaze
the pan. Add the aromatics and stir
until they are fragrant, about 10 to 15
seconds, adjusting the heat so that
they foam in a bubbly mash. Add the
carrots, toss, and cook until half
done, about 1 minute. Add the zucchini, toss well to glaze, then add the
bell pepper and toss to combine.

Stir the liquids, add them to the
pan, bring the mixture to a gentle
simmer, and cover the pan.

Immediately blanch the squid rings
and tentacles in the saucepan of simmering water for only 4 seconds.
Drain promptly.

When the carrots are nearly
cooked, turn off the heat. Stir the
cornstarch mixture to recombine it
and add it to the pan. Stir until the
sauce is glossy, about 10 seconds.
Fold in the drained squid, toss quickly
to combine the ingredients, turn out
onto a heated platter, and serve
immediately.

FLOSSIE VENCE
Aunt Kizzy's Back Porch · Marina del Rey

When she was thirteen Flossie Vence began cooking, in Mississippi, with her grandmother, who was a cook in the sheriff's home. At the age of eighteen she took her first job as a broiler cook at Michael's Café in Cleveland, Mississippi. She cooked fish and steak—American staples—for fifteen years. She also learned more about Southern and Creole foods.

She gained more responsibility when she went to work with the Colonial Inn in Cleveland, Mississippi, where she was asked to open a new restaurant, which meant training the cooks and developing the menu, as well as managing the crew. Flossie continued to work at the Colonial Inn until her children asked her to come to California in 1981.

Flossie Vence

Together, they opened Flossie's in Palos Verdes. It quickly became successful. The menu offered the same kind of food that Flossie had been preparing in Mississippi—chicken pot pie, smothered pork chops, baked beef short ribs, and sweet potato pie.

In 1985, Adolf and Mary Dulan, social workers turned restaurateurs, asked Flossie to be the chef at their newly opened Aunt Kizzy's Back Porch. If success can be judged by the Sunday afternoon line of people trying to get in the door and the favorable newspaper restaurant reviews, Kizzy's has made it. Flossie contends that it has nothing to do with the food. "The Holy Spirit blesses them coming in, and blesses them going out," she says. Success is in the eye of the beholder.

MRS. FLOSSIE'S HUSH PUPPIES

SERVES TWO TO THREE

2 cups white cornmeal
1 teaspoon baking powder
1 medium-sized onion, chopped fine, or
*   several green onions, using both*
*   bottoms and tops*
1 cup milk, more if needed
4 tablespoons shortening, melted
½ teaspoon salt
2 eggs, well beaten

Mix all ingredients to the consistency of a very thick pancake batter. Drop by rounded teaspoonfuls into deep hot fat. Fry until golden brown. Serve hot with fried fish or chicken.

Makes 8 to 10 Hush Puppies.

SYLVIA WU
Madame Wu's Garden · Santa Monica

"In 1962, when I first opened my restaurant in Santa Monica, it accommodated forty people, and I was worried that I would not be able to keep it filled every night. Luckily, among my first patrons were Cary Grant and Lawrence Welk, who helped spread the word.

"It wasn't long before I had to enlarge, taking over an area next door. As time went on, that too became inadequate. I was in a quandary; no more space seemed available. Luck must have been with me, though, because a much larger restaurant a few blocks away was put up for sale. Needless to say, I pounced on it.

"The building needed extensive renovation so, holding my breath, I asked my bank for a half-million dollar loan. I had plenty of sleepless nights wondering how I'd ever pay back all that money, as well as finding enough people to fill the three hundred seats. Happily, the restaurant became a gathering place for theatrical, social, and professional people.

"What makes a restaurant successful? I think the answer is threefold: top-quality food offered in an attractive ambience; excellent service; and a good, sustained public-relations pro-

Sylvia Wu

gram, especially in metropolitan areas where there is heavy competition. I believe, also, that it's important for a restaurant to have a personal identification, with the owner or the host always on hand to welcome guests. I do this myself and, instead of finding it tiresome, to me it's more like having a party every night, greeting the people you like."

179

WHOLE WINTER MELON SOUP

When served impressively with the whole melon cut out as a tureen, this soup is worthy of a banquet.

1 winter melon, about 10 inches high
1 can chicken broth
2 cans water
1 cup uncooked, diced, white chicken
   meat
1/4 cup canned lotus seeds
1/4 cup diced Virginia ham
1/4 cup canned bamboo shoots, diced
1/4 cup canned abalone, diced

Wash the melon and slice off the lid about 3 inches from the stem. Scoop out the seeds and pulp from the center. Make "tiger teeth" notches about 3/4-inch deep around the rim of the melon and pare off the outer skin from the teeth. Cut the fleshy part into small pieces for the soup. Place the melon in an oven-proof bowl and set aside.

Place the chicken broth, water, chicken meat, lotus seeds, ham, and bamboo shoots into the melon.

Pour about 3 inches of boiling water into the bottom of a deep kettle that is large enough to hold the melon. If you have a rack with lift-out handles, put the bowl with the winter melon on it. If not, a simple Chinese method is to place a kitchen towel in the bottom of the kettle, place the bowl on the towel, and bring up the four corners over the melon. Then, you can simply lift out the melon in its bowl by the four corners of the towel.

Cover and steam the melon over medium heat for 2 hours. After 1 hour, check to see if the water level is still at 3 inches; if it is not, add boiling water. When the melon is done, the white meat on its lining will be translucent.

Just before serving, add the abalone and steam for 1 minute.

When serving the soup, scoop the flesh carefully from the sides of the melon, being sure not to cut through the rind.

MISCELLANY

WOMEN IN CUISINE: MÈRE OR CHEF?

BY JANE GRIGSON

A PARTICULARLY IRRITATING PASSAGE in a *Gault-Millau* article a couple of years ago set me thinking about women in the professional kitchen. The subject of the article was the founding of ARC, the French *Association des restauratrices et cuisinières*. The space devoted to it was generous. What I objected to was a corralling of women into the historic category of "*mères*," those rounded matriarchs who ran many of the best restaurants in Lyon for generations. *Gault-Millau's mères* were expected to be earth-mothers, guardians of the territory, while the men got on with the big time. "Here you are, *chère mère*, in this idyllic setting, shelling peas by the mill stream, with dogs/cats/hens/children/geese playing round your feet among the daisies! Why worry your pretty/venerable little heads about guide book ratings, profitable fringe activities, uniformed doormen with your name across their caps?"

Why indeed? I can tell them why. Because for better or worse the heights of the profession, and esteem as well as hard cash, do not lie with willows and rustic *omelettes*. Women with ambition do not want to be everybody's *Mère*—or even *Maîtresse*. They want to be *Chef*. In other words, they want to be chief, recognizably in control.

The *Observer Magazine* agreed to let me explore these matters. I went to see a dozen women chefs in Europe and America. All of them had a reputation anyone might envy. The one I felt closest to, mentally, was Dominique Nahmias, of Olympe, in Paris. She was a shaping influence of the *nouvelle cuisine*, perhaps by chance rather than decision, but she hadn't jibbed at the position she found herself in. She told me she had refused to join ARC. She sees why it has been formed, but feels cooks should not be categorized by sex. "There are good cooks and bad cooks, and a range in between. That's all! What has sex to do with it?"

My first piece was about Joyce Molyneux, of the Carved Angel at Dartmouth, in Devon, one of Britain's most loved and respected restaurants. Her training was ten years hard, with an admirable, demanding chef of the Escoffier school. She began in tears (her domestic science course had not taught her how to section an orange) but learned every skill of the trade, at first with gritted teeth, then with gratitude. Enlightenment came when she worked for George Perry-Smith, at Bath, who cooked with one eye on Elizabeth David's books, the other on the quality of his menu. "Real cooking in a white-washed room," as a fellow disciple put it.

Lydia Shire was another tough professional. I met her at the Bostonian, opposite Faneuil Market, where she was in charge of all the food service. She is, I think, the only woman chef to have complete charge—restaurant, private function catering, breakfasts, room service. Now she has gone to an even larger job on the West Coast. *Chef* she undoubtedly is.

The third chef who had been through the system was Anne Rosenzweig, of New York's Arcadia restaurant. She began as an anthropologist, realized she wanted to cook, and went to work for a chef who had never employed women before. To him women were *mères* with a small *m*. Anne is delicate looking and tiny. No doubt he expected to eat her, *meunière*, for lunch. She stood firm and learned. Her food has a special quality of combining elegance and full flavor. In a blind tasting of dishes, I would defy anyone to pick out hers as "feminine," let alone "motherly."

The rest of my women had been self-taught, perhaps with brief stages at some famous restaurant. They had walked round the system, in one case round bitter parental opposition as well, and got on with it. I think success has surprised them. Alice Waters is the star of this group, and the star of American chefs. She began with Elizabeth David, Pagnol and the south of France, and friendship when she opened Chez Panisse in Berkeley. She had to learn how to make soup for ten, twenty, and thirty, and why a restaurant is not the same as an open house for friends.

Of the women chefs I saw, most were working in a family setup. This is sometimes held against them—"dinner parties for paying guests"—though not against men, which is odd. A couple sets out to run a restaurant; if the man is the cook all goes with a swing. I think of Marc Meneau, of St-Père-sous-Vezelay. If it's the woman in the kitchen, attitudes are different. She is less likely, for a start, to gain the recognition of hieratic male chefs and their professional associations, which will in the end accommodate mavericks, if they are men. Luckily it is the public, and untrained food journalists, who bring success, not the framed diplomas on the wall. Would women not be wise to exploit this kind of support more than they do, while resisting categorization on any grounds other than merit? Of course merit is not always justly assessed, but that is a problem for men as well. Merit of at least a minimum kind is what the word *chef* implies: it can accommodate everyone who earns it. *Mère* is a condition that can only befall 50 percent of the human race, which makes it too emotional in its implications by far.

Jane Grigson is a celebrated food authority from Great Britain and writer of several outstanding cookbooks.

A MOST DIFFICULT
BUSINESS

BY JOYCE GOLDSTEIN

IF YOU ARE A GOOD COOK, it is inevitable that some well-meaning friend has said to you with the afterglow of wine and the taste of your succulent *boeuf bourguignon* on his lips: "You know, you should open a restaurant." Ah, the siren song! However, before you take that step and turn a pleasurable hobby into a full-time business, you ought to consider the ramifications of such a career move and see if you are really cut out for the work.

There are two words that best describe the restaurant business (if you have any chance of being in the business for a while). Those words are "relentless" and "consistent."

By "relentless" I mean it never goes away, and neither do you. If two cooks are out sick, you don't say to customers, "Well, we had to prepare fewer dishes today because we are shorthanded."

No, you work harder and longer and so do the other cooks so that no one knows that things are not in perfect order. You cannot afford to ease up on anyone. You must taste everything. You must see that the plates go out looking good. You must see that the waiting staff are neat in appearance. You must check to see if the janitors cleaned the spots on the ceiling. You must call the electricians, and then call them again because they forgot. Of course you can delegate some things away. But the buck stops with you, if there are to be any bucks at all.

Forget about the social life: You won't have much, because you are married to your restaurant. Of course, you can take an occasional night off, even a long weekend, and eventually a vacation for a few weeks (almost guilt-free), but you can't stay away too long or too often and expect to have the place running smoothly.

Which leads to "consistent." You are reviewed every day, not always by food writers, but by your customers, both new and old. You cannot let up on quality for one minute.

"Good enough" may be good enough for others, but not for you, if you take pride in your work. People come to expect a certain level of expertise, a certain style, good ingredients, the same level of competent service, cleanliness, all sorts of amenities that you didn't know that they had noticed, until the moment that you lapse, and they are quick to point out your shortcomings. You are only as good as their last dinner in your restaurant.

Are you financially savvy? Because understanding budgets and balance sheets is just as important as knowing how to cook a perfect *beurre blanc*. In this business, money rears its ugly head right from the inception, and it never goes away.

More often than not, these days, where restaurants are reviewed as environments, too much is spent in construction, art works and fancy *décor*, fat design and legal fees called "pre-opening costs"—dollars that may never be recouped. If you spent too much up front, you may not see black ink for years. So you must be careful to budget your dollars. You can buy artworks later on, or fancy china and glassware. But good kitchen equipment and a well-stocked small wine cellar are sound investments.

Avoid fads. Cook what you know. If you just follow the trends of the moment, your restaurant may be passé before it is established. And study your market. Does your neighborhood need another Cajun restaurant or mesquite grill?

Hire people whose palate you can trust, and who think about food the way you do. But don't hire yes-men in management and financial planning. Get people on your staff who will disagree with you, and challenge you so that you may learn from their experience and, perhaps, stay in business.

Cost your menu items. Don't guess what the right price may be. Study menus from other places that are similar to yours in concept and price range. Work with your purveyors to get the best prices. Have alternate sources of supply whenever possible. Complain. Keep your eyes open. Select the right equipment and kitchen layout for the kind of food you plan to serve. Be flexible and open-minded but don't get talked into lots of fancy gadgets and overly technological expensive equipment that you don't really need.

I don't mean to sound gloomy and pessimistic, but this is a brutal business, with an alarming rate of failure. If you think that running a restaurant is glamorous, you may be rudely surprised. For every moment of glamor, excitement, and creativity there are hours of drudgery, and hard physical and mental work.

If you do not have lots of stamina, a single-mindedness of purpose, the ability to make decisions under pressure, choose another career. In fact, if you are not driven, and do not breathe, eat, and sleep "pressure," don't enter this field. People who love the restaurant business love that feeling of living on the edge, the constant tension, the pressure to get the food out and ready on time. They thrive on difficult odds. (Line cooks, waiters, and hosts are bored on slow nights and are happiest and at their best when they are racing.) Cooking is only a meditation when you are peeling a thousand cloves of garlic. The rest of the time it is high-speed high-wire work.

So why do some of us do it? Believe it or not, it's not the money. You probably could do better with a good job and a money market account. Fame and glory are fleeting at best, often distracting and debilitating. We do it because we are hooked. Restaurant work is addictive, habit forming. We do it because we need to hear, "That was really delicious." "We had a wonderful evening; you made us feel so at home." "We'll be back soon and we'll tell all our friends." "This is my favorite restaurant."

Ah, that is the food for our souls. It is ego, too. It is art. It is making paintings that people devour. It is theater that receives a rave review. It's fun only if you are suited to the game, and the game is rough.

Hundreds of new restaurants open each year, and most of them fail. Some of those that fail may even have good food! They may suffer from poor management, poor location, bad press. Others may not catch on because they never felt hospitable, or because the service was terrible, or snooty, or sloppy. Or because the owners were never there and all sorts of short cuts were taken. Or because they weren't trendy. Or because they were trendy. Because they were too good but never found an audience. Because they were not discovered soon enough before they ran out of money.

There are all sorts of reasons, and you rarely know why. So you must be prepared to take the big risk, if you decide to enter the business. If you don't like the heat, stay out of the restaurant kitchen.

SHE WORKS HARD FOR THE GLORY

BY WILLIAM RICE

*"Fellow workers!" she shouted at the cooks. "Your
cooking lacks awareness. Because you refuse to recognize
for centuries the male cook was a product of the
monasteries and courts, in other words, of the ruling class.
We female cooks, on the other hand, have always served
the people. In our ranks there are . . . no famous chefs."*

From *The Flounder* by Günter Grass

LIKE SO MANY OTHER examples of sexual stratification, this one is history. In the United States of the late nineteen eighties, women chefs are a reality: in demand, prospering and—in some cases—even famous. A survey by the Chicago Tribune of women chefs in Chicago and several other key cities across the nation reveals the following: Opportunities for women cooks in the food service industry are "virtually unlimited," according to a leading restaurant consultant. Great strides have been made in removing sexual barriers and reducing sexual harassment of women who choose careers as professional cooks. In perhaps no other country is the equal opportunity kitchen as much a reality as in the United States.

Despite this favorable climate and the greatly increased status of cooking as a profession, there has been a leveling off of the percentage of women entering the field. A variety of psychological and physical barriers are cited as reasons why, in the years ahead, women chefs probably will not become as prevalent as women lawyers or MBAs.

Chefs of the caliber of Leslee Reis (Café Provençal, Leslee's, and Bodega Bay), Carolyn Buster (The Cottage), Jackie Shen (Jackie's), and Monique

Hooker (Monique's Café) have propelled Chicago to the forefront of the women chefs' movement. Their achievements have paved the way for other chefs in Chicago, among them Jennifer Newbury of Amerique, Nina Nicolai of the Italian Village's Florentine Room, Jennifer Smith at Cafe Ba-Ba-Reeba! and Susan Weaver at the Ritz-Carlton. Talented women chefs are now equally visible in such diverse locales as New York City, San Francisco, Los Angeles, and Seattle.

The two most dramatic challenges yet for American women chefs are now going on simultaneously on opposite sides of the country. In New York City, Anne Rosenzweig, a diminutive thirty-two-year-old chef who studied anthropology in college, has revised the menu and kitchen team at 21, that venerable bastion of male clubbiness. Meanwhile, Lydia Shire, who, at thirty-nine is the mother of three children as well as a veteran chef, has been given command of the kitchens of the new Four Seasons Hotel in Los Angeles. She is thought to be the first female executive chef of a major chain hotel. Highly visible jobs, both of them. Neither woman is a singular "token" or supervisor of a station. She's the ultimate boss of a hundred or more employees. "What Anne and Lydia are doing represents a new dimension, a change in scale," says Joseph Baum, who created such New York restaurant monuments as the Four Seasons and Windows on the World. "Their success will mean all the barriers will be down."

There is no precise chronicle of women's progress as professional cooks in the United States. As in Europe, women cooked with distinction and ran inns and restaurants at various times in all parts of the country. The first woman chef to emerge with the so-called gourmet food boom of the nineteen sixties was Julia Child, "the French Chef." Child is neither French nor a chef. She is an American-born, French-trained teacher, not a professional cook. But her vast personal popularity and strong support of women cooks made a great difference.

It was the early seventies before Alice Waters, who has become the doyenne of modern American women chefs, opened Chez Panisse, her now-famous restaurant in Berkeley. About the same time, in 1972, the Culinary

Institute of America, the nation's leading academic training ground for cooks, admitted three women, its first female students. A decade later, Carlyn Berghoff of the Chicago restaurant family became the first female student council president at the CIA. Now women make up between a quarter and a third of the nation's student cooks.

Whatever launched the female invasion of male-ruled restaurant kitchens, it is being fueled by necessity. Dining out has become such an important facet of the American way of life that the industry now has about a hundred thousand entry-level jobs to fill each year. Graduates of prominent culinary training schools can anticipate multiple job offers, starting salaries of $18,000 to $20,000 or higher, and the possibility of reaching the $40,000-to-$50,000 range within five years.

That so many of these graduates are women comes as a surprise to many old-line chefs and restaurant customers. "When the chef of our Fuller's restaurant (Kathy Casey) comes into the dining room," says Louis B. Richmond, director of public relations for the Seattle Sheraton Hotel & Towers, "invariably people are startled to discover she is a woman and shocked at how young she looks and is." (Casey is twenty-four. Her *sous chef*, also a woman, is twenty-three.) There have been women chefs before, of course. In France at least one of them, the legendary Mère Brazier of Lyon, even held the Michelin Guide's top, three-star rating in the 1950s. But in general the prevalent attitude toward women chefs in Europe has been a doctrine of separate and unequal that holds to this day. Most women chefs there are born into the business. They inherit a family-owned restaurant or hotel and employ only women cooks in their kitchens.

Chauvinist male chefs—in my experience more fearful of how they would maintain discipline in the kitchen of young male and female cooks than actively hostile to women—cited the physical rigors of the job as the chief reason for excluding them. Those women who won admission were relegated to preparing salads and pastries and kept well away from the stove.

"When I went to Europe in the mid-nineteen seventies," recalls Rozanne Gold, the first chef for New York City's Mayor Ed Koch and now a successful consultant, "people said they felt sorry that, as a woman, I had to do such denigrating work."

Chefs who immigrated to this country brought their antifemale bias with them. A woman cook no longer in the field recalls two incidents during the same period: "I begged for a job at a French restaurant in Chicago," she says. "When the chef finally relented, he said, 'I must ask you two things: Are you really serious about working here? And do you realize I am already married?'" Later, working at a French restaurant in New York, she was given paychecks made out to "*fille*" (girl). The owner made no effort to learn her name. "There was no overt hostility," she says now. "But there was no attempt to teach me anything, either. I had to follow the cooks around and play Twenty Questions to get any information."

Even today, a woman's credibility is very low in many kitchens around the world. Amy Beneccki, chef-consultant for the Levy Organization here, reports that on a recent trip to Asia she was stopped and questioned twice during visits to kitchens. "They asked if I had made up the information on my business card," she says. "They wouldn't believe I was really a chef. In the kitchens I visited there were no female cooks. The only women I encountered were sweeping floors."

In this country, however, the current view is that male chauvinism in the kitchen is largely a generational problem. "Our female students are aware that the professional kitchen has been a male domain and that they may encounter difficulties," says Ann Faulkner of the Culinary School of Kendall College in suburban Evanston. "But they are as enthusiastic as our male students and may have a more focused view of what they want to achieve." Elsewhere in Chicago, women graduates of Washburn Trade School and the Cooking and Hospitality Institute have successfully made the transition to professional kitchens in the area.

Dorothy Cann, director of the French Culinary Institute in New York, says she has used the school's leverage (it is the only culinary school in New York with official blessing from Paris) to gain positions for women graduates with French chefs in the kitchens of such luxury restaurants as Le

Bernardin and La Grenouille. "At first the chefs are reluctant, then they are amazed that a woman can be so good. Once one proves herself, generally there is no problem for women who follow her."

(Everyone interviewed in connection with this article reported that in restaurants across the country with open-minded young chefs—both American and French—male and female cooks are working side-by-side with excellent rapport and outstanding results. The most prevalent complaint now is that there are not enough women to go into all the kitchens that want them. Leslee Reis, for example, says she has yet to have enough trained women available to reach a 50-50 male-female balance in the kitchen at Café Provençal.)

Inevitably, there are claims that not only can women hold their own, but they may be superior to their male counterparts in the kitchen. Among qualities ascribed to women chefs, some by males are: "very competitive, more driven to succeed," "more creative," "more adaptable," "greater sensitivity," "more detail-oriented, far more perfectionist," "quicker to look around for work to be done," "they get sick less."

"To me, women working on the line have a lighter touch and move a little differently than men," says Kathy Casey. "They are more choreographed. My *sous chef* is the best example I know. She moves softly and lifts food so gently she might be picking up a butterfly. She doesn't make a lot of moves, she just makes the right ones."

Not surprisingly, all the above attributes are disputed—even among women—as not being exclusively or predominantly female. But Ferdinand Metz, president of the CIA, offers an impressive testimonial to the abilities of the female students who attend his school. "Women make up only about 25 percent of the enrollment," he says, "but they win about 80 percent of the awards in each graduating class. There is a lot of quality there."

William Rice is the Food Editor of The Chicago Tribune.

A SKETCH
OF TWO CATERERS

*Gloria Steinem says that the last frontier women have to
cross is the financial one. I think I've crossed it.*

Andrea Bell

MANY AMERICAN WOMEN are great cooks. Few are great chefs. Isn't there anything in between? Some would answer, catering, seeing that as an important transition, a bridge, between home and restaurant kitchens. (Gerri Gilliland at Gilliland's restaurant began her professional career as a caterer.) Others assert that catering is best viewed as an end in itself.

Hermine Harman has recently entered the food profession: She catered her first meal a month before this writing. She considers that meal a fabulous success but also an important learning experience. What got her to that first meal?

Hermine grew up in a food-centered environment. Her grandfather founded, owned, and ran a delicatessen in Los Angeles. Her father took over the family business at the age of sixteen. He was certainly what Hermine terms a "foodie." He taught his young wife the basics of cooking, then supported her development to the status of "outstanding" cook. Meal time was *the* time in Hermine's childhood.

Hermine's first husband was an artist. They ate their way through Europe, studying each regional cuisine. Hermine eventually returned to Los Angeles, divorced the artist, and began a career in medical social work. She met her current husband Alvin while setting up a hospice care program for his dying mother.

Hermine traveled to Vienna with Alvin in March, 1980, so that he could join an East-West think tank known as the International Institute for Applied Systems Analysis. The Institute was housed in one of the summer castles of the Hapsburgs. It was also largely male.

The scientists' wives instituted a Women's Club, of which Hermine soon became president. Throughout her tenure, she organized numerous major social events for the Club. An American Thanksgiving dinner, for the entire multinational institute, had Hermine stuffing twenty-six imported turkeys. She also took cooking classes in the castle, and always laughs as she remembers learning to make flour *tortillas* in Austria.

The Harmans returned to Los Angeles in September, 1981. Three months later Alvin underwent major surgery. The initial trauma of the operation was followed by extended months of stress. Having to nurse a man who would not be able to return to work for over three years, Hermine realized that she would have to leave medical work and find another profession. In the meantime, she had turned her hand to volunteer work. For three years she worked on special events for the Municipal Elections Committee of Los Angeles and then joined (and soon became president of) the Board of Directors of the Los Angeles Woman's Building.

In 1986, Hermine offered to do the food for the Board's Christmas party. That spontaneous act of generosity led her to turn a professional corner. So many at the party exclaimed that they would love to have her "do" a party for them, that she determined to find a way to develop parties for a profit. She enrolled in the Professional Practices of Catering Program at the University of California, Los Angeles, had cards and stationery printed, and sent letters to every friend and acquaintance whose current address she had. She decided to offer spa cuisine as well as international cuisine so that her food would have particular appeal to the health conscious.

Hermine regrets that she undercharged—by between $10 and $15 a head—for that first party. And she regrets that she did it in partnership with another caterer. (She's sure, in retrospect, that this partnership was largely inspired by insecurity.) But the food was good; the party successful. And from it, she booked two large parties, and a series of small "very gourmet" dinners. Where will Hermine go with all this? If she's lucky—and determined—she might go in some of the directions taken by Andrea Bell.

Andrea Bell is one of the most highly lauded caterers in the country. Her L.A. Celebrations has received national and international news coverage; she plans many dozens of major celebrity events a year.

Like Hermine, Andrea grew up in a food-oriented household. "My entire family has a passion for food. On both sides!" Cooking has been her great love since childhood. She remembers winning a cooking contest in grammar school. "Actually, I got second place—my best friend won first place. But she used a cake mix and just added some stuff to it. I started from scratch!" Starting from scratch is still Andrea's priority: The first tenet of her published objectives for catering is "*Quality*—to provide the highest quality cuisine available—including the freshest produce, seafood, prime meats, sweet butter, etc."

Like Hermine, Andrea began adult life intending to enter the medical or social services field. While pursuing her Masters Degree in Psychology at Boston University, she worked as food editor for the *New Age Journal*. She also traveled in Europe, India, and the Middle East, studying regional cooking. She would return from each extended trip and offer classes in what her wanderings had taught her.

While in Boston, Andrea studied with Madeleine Kamman, whom she describes as being, "like a mother who is as loving as she is stern . . . the strongest influence in my professional career. Madeleine sets such high standards of expectations for her students that you almost don't feel you can meet them."

Andrea has also studied Moroccan cuisine with Paula Wolfert; *nouvelle cuisine* with Jacques Pépin, Nancy Silverton, and Jonathan Waxman; bread making with James Beard. She has studied at the Cordon Bleu and at l'École de Cuisine La Varenne, in Paris, and with Mrs. Balbir Singh in New Delhi, India. In 1978, she and a partner founded the still successful Formaggio Kitchen in Cambridge, Massachusetts. In spite of her impressive résumé, when she applied for jobs at "all the top restaurants in Los Angeles," no one would take her except at minimum wage.

Andrea came to Los Angeles to pursue a doctorate degree in psychology, thinking that she would cook to support her academic endeavors. She began to cook for the "rich and famous," for everyone from movie moguls to Arab sheiks. And she did a little catering on the side, on weekends.

Then she got two major breaks. One of her last cooking clients was Brenda Vaccaro, who let Andrea cook for her every day she needed to (that is, enough to support herself and pay her tuition expenses), and was tremendously supportive—"a cheerleader!"—whenever Andrea had the chance to cater a party. By 1981, Andrea was thinking that, if she could do two really good-sized parties a month, she could support herself.

Someone gave her name to the Los Angeles Olympic Organizing Committee, and she found herself one of many caterers in Los Angeles competing to do a lunch for Prince Philip, Duke of Edinburgh. At this time, Andrea was still cooking out of her small kitchen at home. She had to use the address of a friend's croissant shop as she filled out application forms for the Committee.

"I tend," said Andrea, "to really rise to challenges. I tend to do overkill to make things perfect." By all accounts, lunch for Prince Philip *was* perfect—in spite of the fact that she had cooked throughout the night before, in order to have the pastries and breads as fresh as possible; in spite of the fact that a warning light went on in her VW Rabbit as she drove the food from her kitchen in Los Angeles down to San Diego; in spite of the fact that the Prince arrived twenty minutes early and the meal, which had been scheduled literally to the minute for each course, had to be rapidly accelerated during the crucial last half hour of cooking.

Since her Olympic "coming out," the fame of Andrea Bells' L.A. Celebrations has risen meteorically. She has done everything from buffet dinners for five thousand guests to intimate dinners for five. She once did a dinner for sixteen hundred people in honor of Gerald Ford, on an undeveloped cliff overlooking the ocean in Newport Beach. She coordinated everything from tents to bathrooms—and, of course, the food. In the hallway of their fancy office building, she did a dinner for the Board of Trustees of a major corporation, setting up a portable kitchen in the mailroom and using a camouflaged copying machine for a bar. More recently, she did a 150th Birthday Party for the "Dynasty" television program, a party that was clearly intended to be a media event. She does museum openings. She develops entire party concepts for people in Georgia, Florida, New York, and Washington, D.C.

Her catering business no longer works out of anyone's home kitchen. In 1985, she bought an old warehouse on Robertson Boulevard, gutted it, and built four kitchens. She leases the three small kitchens to a French pastry chef, a *chocolatier*, and a brownie maker. Out of the fourth, she runs her business with a staff of two hundred full- and part-time members.

Asked when she decided to leave psychology for a full-time commitment to catering, she answers, without hesitation: "When I realized I was really supporting myself well." Then she adds, "I deal in joy now. In psychology, for the most part, you deal in pain . . . but my psychological background certainly has enabled me to work with people on occasions which are for the most part joyous, but also stressful . . . like birthdays, or Christmas. I do a lot of hand holding.

"I really try to understand what my clients want. I try to tailor each event to bring across their tastes, whether they are especially health conscious, or eclectic and willing to experiment. I think I can really hear what they are saying."

Andrea herself deals with every client and goes to every party—as many as three or four a night. All of her business has been publicized by word of mouth; over 80 percent of it is repeat business. Asked why she has had so few problems in the light of such splendid success, she asserts that she always tried to be true to herself, in terms of attention to quality. As for advice for future caterers, she sighs, "It's hard. You have to be extremely dedicated. You have to have a lot of integrity. You have to be an enormously hard worker. (She remembers that in her high school of more than three thousand students, she received the award for the "Hardest Worker.") I don't think I had a single day off for the first three years of my business. It's a service business. You have to be there to serve your clients, no matter what. I feel I have achieved a lot. I've come home; I can use all my skills. I want to continue doing exactly what I'm doing for the rest of my career."

NEW BOONEVILLE
REVISITED

ONE BEAUTIFUL SPRING AFTERNOON, Charlene Rollins pointed to some rare *Caville Blanc d'Hiver* apple saplings. The young trees were planted between the New Boonville Hotel and the restaurant's famed produce garden. "Planting this many fruit trees is a sign of our commitment," she said. "We'll be here to harvest them. A lot of people think we're crazy. We intend to be here until we die." That was in 1983. By November 1986, Charlene and her husband and partner, Vernon, were in a pickup truck making a getaway down the country highway from creditors, auditors, lawyers, and the police. They were, and still are, fugitives from the law, characterized by some as merely bad business people with an idealistic dream and by others as frauds.

What they left behind—the New Boonville Hotel, Restaurant and Bar—will not be forgotten in the California restaurant world, nor should it be taken lightly by those who dream of owning their own restaurant. The Rollinses fled when Charlene was seven months into her pregnancy. She had worked as chef up until the last day. Her schedule, as well as Vernon's, had been one of brutally long hours—six days a week for two years. As Vernon wrote in a letter, which included some of the back wages he owed his employees, to a local newspaper, "Work fifteen, sixteen, twenty hours a day; sleep; get up and do it again. Never paid ourselves, sold our possessions to finance the place. No, nothing except work, sleep, work. Talk to lawyers, deal with creditors, work, sleep."

Their legacy included six trust deeds worth over $500,000 against the hotel, twenty misdemeanor violations of the state labor code (the head waiter claimed that they owed about him $18,000 in back tips and wages), a legendary garden overgrown with weeds and a stack of laudatory reviews of their restaurant clipped from publications that ranged from *Esquire* to the *Los Angeles Times*.

The Rollins's story is the nightmare side of celebrity, where images collide with reality, and fame outdistances tangible success. In the end, it was not a pretty picture.

Charlene's involvement with food had begun years earlier, when she received a copy of Julia Child's landmark cookbook, *Mastering the Art of French Cooking*, as a Book-of-the-Month-Club dividend. She became so engrossed in cooking that she left college to volunteer at Chez Panisse in Berkeley. Alice Waters has said about her former protégée, "Charlene can be very ambitious. She picks the parsley from the garden the moment the dish is ordered. I appreciate that, although it would drive me crazy."

Charlene's first paying kitchen job was at the Café Mozart in San Francisco. While working there, she began to search for a place of her own, a plan that took on further momentum when she met Vernon at a party. They both wanted to own their own restaurant.

The search led to a rundown hotel with a garbage dump behind it in the middle of the Anderson Valley, a rural area known for its apples, pears, and grapes. The couple acquired some cash from a number of investors, most of whom were also friends, and bought the New Boonville Hotel. The name was not their invention. The hotel was originally one of a string built by Wells Fargo to accommodate travelers and horses. Every twenty-seven miles along the coastal route, there was another way station. The original hotel burned down and was replaced by the "new" one in the mid-eighteen nineties.

At first the plan was to renovate the hotel, install a tennis court and swimming pool, and to have a gourmet restaurant with a menu based entirely on locally grown products. Much of the restaurant's mystique would later come from the claim that most of the food was grown in the New Boonville's large kitchen garden. Employees later said that, in fact, most of the food was not grown on the premises, but was bought from a variety of sources, such as a produce market in Ukiah, twenty-five miles away.

The restaurant opened in February 1982; the rest of the renovations were postponed indefinitely. The restaurant drew social climbers and gastronomes to the valley, to the exclusion, some felt, of the local people. The parking lot would be full of expensive automobiles not normally seen in sleepy Boonville. As the restaurant's justifiable fame grew, so did the numbers of visitors who made the pilgrimage from San Francisco, 125 miles south. Finally, the New Boonville was discovered by the press.

When they received a notice that they had been given a culinary award by *Cook's* magazine, the Rollinses just laughed. "Who has the time or money to go to New York to receive an award?" they asked. Now their old kitchen is boarded up, Charlene and Vernon were last reported to be somewhere in France, and it's hard to imagine that the New Boonville ever caused such a stir.

Some say the fault was in New Boonville's poor management, and Vernon's labyrinthine mortgaging, by which he would borrow money from new creditors to pay, in part, what he owed the old investors. Others contend that it was the creditors themselves who were shortsighted, and did not give the uncompromising Rollinses a chance to realize their dream of having the perfect restaurant. Certainly the reasons for failure were many and diverse, but still the Rollinses left their mark on the California restaurant world—and the apple saplings continue to grow in Anderson Valley.

HERB SALAD

Although the herbs have been specified in this recipe, the salad may be made with any herb that does not have too distinctive a flavor—sage comes to mind as one to be avoided.

2 tablespoons green leaf basil
2 tablespoons opal basil
2 tablespoons lemon basil
2 tablespoons Thai cinnamon basil
2 tablespoons tarragon
2 tablespoons sweet marjoram
2 tablespoons coriander leaves
2 tablespoons flat-leaf (Italian) parsley
2 cups lettuce, washed and separated
4 large eggs, 3 to 4 days old
1 red tomato
1 yellow tomato
1 red onion, sweet and small
1 cup milk
4 pickled gherkins, or pickled green beans
½ cup Parmesan, or other hard cheese, at room temperature
½ cup olive oil
⅙ cup red wine vinegar
1 tablespoon unsweetened mustard
Pinch ground black pepper

Pick all the herb leaves off their stems. Wash, along with the lettuce, and towel dry. Boil the eggs for 5 to 6 minutes and immerse them in cold water. Peel the eggs, and cut them into ½-inch chunks (they will be runny). Skin, seed, juice, and dice the tomatoes. Slice the red onion as thinly as possible (a slicer is recommended) and soak the slices in the milk. Drain them thoroughly before using.

Dice the gherkins or green beans. Grate the cheese through the largest holes on the grater. Make a mustard vinaigrette by combining the olive oil, vinegar, and unsweetened mustard.

Put the dry herbs and lettuce in a bowl with the vinaigrette and the other ingredients. Mix very well, coating all the leaves. Serve on chilled salad plates and top each salad with a grind of black pepper. This salad goes well with rabbit *terrine*.

CHICORY CHOWDER

1 head chicory
6 slices cured and smoked bacon
1 tablespoon butter
2 small red onions
4 tablespoons flour
4 small waxy potatoes
1 ripe bell pepper, minced
1 cup rich chicken stock
2 cups milk
2 cups heavy cream
Salt and pepper
Pinch allspice
Pinch cayenne pepper
2 tablespoons flat-leaf (Italian) parsley, chopped

Discard the outer leaves of the chicory, and cut out the stem of each inner leaf. Cut the stems into small dice, and the leaves into *chiffonade* strips, keeping them separate.

Mince 4 slices of the bacon and cook them in the butter until the fat is rendered. Dice the red onions, and sweat them in the fat. Sprinkle in the flour and cook for a few minutes, stirring. Add the potatoes, bell pepper, chicken stock, milk, and heavy cream. Bring to a simmer and add the chicory stems. Cook for 5 minutes. Add the chicory leaves, and cook for an additional 5 minutes.

Season with the salt, pepper, allspice, and cayenne. Garnish with the remaining 2 slices of bacon, cooked crisp, chopped finely, and mixed with the chopped flat-leaf parsley.

FRESH NOODLES WITH RABBIT INNARDS & RED PEPPERS

The roasted rabbit is optional: It may be served with the noodles or you may use the innards for this dish and reserve the rabbit itself for another meal.

1 rabbit (reserve the innards for the sauce)
3 red bell peppers
1 cup good, mild olive oil
1 large sweet red onion, finely sliced
6 cloves garlic, finely chopped
3 tablespoons fresh tarragon leaves (reserve a few sprigs)
1 pound fresh egg noodles

Roast the rabbit whole in a 400°F oven for 25 minutes. Cut the rabbit into 6 portions, using a cleaver to split the backbone. Reserve the juices. Keep warm while you prepare the sauce. (Or, if you do not wish to serve the rabbit, simply reserve the innards when you cook a rabbit for some other meal.)

Char, seed, and peel the bell peppers, reserving the juices, and cut them into thin slices. Pour the olive oil into a sauté pan and gently cook the onion until limp, but still pink. Add the garlic and cook briefly. Turn off the heat and add the peppers and juices, tarragon leaves, and innards.

Cook the noodles for thirty seconds, while re-heating the contents of the sauté pan. The innards will cook very quickly. Drain the noodles and add them to the sauté pan, tossing to mix. Turn the noodles out on a large platter, and reassemble the rabbit on top. Decorate the platter with tarragon sprigs.

GRILLED LEEKS WITH BACON & CAPER CREAM SAUCE

SERVES TWO

4 leeks
Salt
Black pepper
¼ cup clarified butter
2 slices cured, smoked bacon
¼ tablespoon garlic, finely chopped
1 tablespoon capers, roughly chopped
½ to ¾ cup heavy cream
1 tablespoon flat-leaf (Italian) parsley, freshly chopped

Clean and blanch the leeks, with the roots left on but trimmed, until they are tender but still intact. Drain well and grill over a mesquite and fruitwood fire until lightly toasted on the outside and creamy on the inside. As they grill, season them with salt and pepper, and baste with clarified butter.

To make the sauce, mince the bacon and cook it in a sauté pan until rendered and lightly crisped. Add the garlic and stir over a low heat until cooked but not browned. Add the capers, heavy cream, black pepper, and flat-leaf parsley.

Reduce until smooth, but not too thick. Cut the leeks into one-inch pieces with a sharp knife. Reassemble on a warm plate and spoon the sauce over the center of the leeks.

MASHED POTATOES WITH
PEPPERMINT & GARLIC CHIVES

12 medium waxy potatoes, either red or yellow
Pinch salt
1⅓ cups cream
2 tablespoons coarsely chopped peppermint
2 tablespoons sliced or snipped garlic chives

Peel the potatoes, quarter them, and immediately immerse them in cold water to keep them white. Cook the potatoes in a saucepan of salted, simmering, water until they are just cooked through, but not soft or crumbly. Drain and cover them with cold water.

In a few minutes, drain again and refrigerate until cold. Then put them through a fine grater attachment on any mixer, keeping the potatoes as light and uncompacted as possible.

Put the cream into a nonstick sauté pan. Add the potatoes, peppermint, and garlic chives. Salt and pepper liberally (using freshly ground pepper). Cook, stirring, mashing, and whipping with a wooden spoon, until the cream in incorporated and the mixture is coherent, although there will still be some tiny "lumps" in the potatoes.

JOSEPHINE ARALDO
A NATIONAL TREASURE

BY ROBERT REYNOLDS

FRENCH COOKS love to give to their dishes names that betray nothing concrete about the dish. Part of the satisfaction is the opportunity to speculate on the gastronomic pleasures the dish itself offers. For example, there is a confection called *Sans Rival*, which means Without Equal. A book about Josephine Araldo might well have that title, for surely it captures something of her singularity.

Josephine's culinary responses come from a source that is now unfamiliar even to many French people. She was born in Brittany in 1895. Her grandmother, La Mère Jacquette, owned a small farm that bordered a dark, shallow river typical of the south coast. "La Mère Jacquette didn't like Napoleon" is something I have heard Josephine say. I turn the phrase over and over in my mind; it's like a smooth stone in my hand in that it gives me a sense of time, over time.

When Henri-Paul Pellaprat, the man who founded the Cordon Bleu, wanted to praise his favorite student, he would tell Josephine that she was a natural cook. Josephine would demur, giving La Mère Jacquette the credit for her culinary outlook. The magic of her grandmother's genius was already part of Josephine's makeup by the time she entered the Cordon Bleu in 1918.

Cooking is a tapestry of vibrant textures. It is peopled in France by individuals of character: Escoffier, Montagné, Pellaprat, and La Mère Jacquette from whose uncomplicated culinary gift so much of the subject derives; and in America, by Josephine, who is a living repository of the subject's greatest events. The subject remains cooking, and at age 93, Josephine is still active, vibrant and very interested in food.

Josephine trained at Cordon Bleu with about forty-five other women. Pellaprat certified her as *chef de cuisine* and later as *chef pâtissière*. This double training, not unheard of, certainly was in character for a woman, born in a small stone house next to the village church, who had a burning desire for education. At the Cordon Bleu she was trained by the best to be the best. Pellaprat found in her a natural talent that was very strong. When he gave her her toque, he told her he was crowning her. She replied, "I don't see any jewels in this crown, Henri." To which he answered: "You are the jewel."

She comes from the southern half of the Breton peninsula—next to a place called Finisterre—the end of the earth. The name is appropriate for the image of one who has been afforded the luxury of imparting the spirit of her profession above all other values. Josephine spends her professional life exemplifying and inspiring a faith in the best; and leaves us the pleasant prospect of regarding her as a National Treasure.

Mr. Reynolds is the chef and owner of Le Trou in San Francisco. His cooking classes with Josephine Araldo attract cooking students, professionals, and home cooks.

CULINARY SOCIETIES
IN THE UNITED STATES
AND COOKING SCHOOLS

CULINARY SOCIETIES

American Institute of Wine and Food
846 California Street
San Francisco, Calif. 94108

San Francisco Professional Food Society
2714 Steiner Street
San Francisco, Calif. 94123

Southern California Culinary Guild
4901 Morena Boulevard, Suite 809
San Diego, Calif. 92117

Women's Culinary Alliance
246 Twenty-sixth Street
Santa Monica, Calif. 90402

Northwest Culinary Alliance
Box 16570
Seattle, Wash. 98116

Houston Women's Culinary Guild
303 Timberwilde
Houston, Tex. 77024

Chicago Culinary Guild
Box 274
Kenilworth, Ill. 60043

Les Dames d'Escoffier, Chicago
1728 Wild Berry Drive
Glenview, Ill. 60025

International Association of Cooking
   Schools
1001 Connecticut Avenue NW
Washington, D.C. 20036

Les Dames d'Escoffier, Washington
2735 P Street NW
Washington D.C. 20007

Culinary Historians of Boston
268 Elm Street
Concord, Mass. 01742

The Women's Culinary Guild
10 Pierrepont Road
Newton, Mass. 02162

Les Dames d'Escoffier, New York
20 East Ninth Street
New York, N.Y. 10003

New York Women's Culinary Alliance
327 West Eighteenth Street
New York, N.Y. 10011

COOKING SCHOOLS

California Culinary Academy
625 Polk Street, Department CKS
San Francisco, Calif. 94118

Culinary Institute of America
Box 9600
Hyde Park, N.Y. 12538

Tante Marie's Cooking School
271 Francisco Street
San Francisco, Calif. 94133

Madeleine Kamman
Private professional instruction
P.O. Box 363
Bartlett, N.H. 03812
and
14 Faubourg des Balmettes
Annecy 7400, France

Martha Stewart's Entertaining Seminars
    in Westport, Connecticut
10 Saugatuck Avenue
Westport, Conn. 06880

The Culinary School of Kendall College
2408 Orrington Avenue
Evanston, Ill. 60201

L'Académie de Cuisine
5021 Wilson Lane
Bethesda, Md. 20814

Baltimore's International Culinary Arts
    Institute
19–21 South Gay Street
Baltimore, Md. 21202

The French Culinary Institute
462 Broadway
New York, N.Y. 10013

International Pastry Arts Center
357 Adams Street
Bedford Hills, N.Y. 10507

Peter Kump's New York Cooking School
307 East Ninety-second Street
New York, N.Y. 10128

Culinary Institute
1316 Southwest Fourteenth
Portland, Oreg. 97201

The Restaurant School
2129 Walnut Street
Philadelphia, Pa. 19103

Memphis Culinary Academy
La Maison Méridien
1252 Peabody Avenue
Memphis, Tenn. 38104

Joyce Jue Cuisine of the Orient
1980 Sutter Street, No. 303
San Francisco, Calif. 94115

The Cordon Bleu Cookery School of
London
114 Marylebone Lane
London, W.1., England

Flavors of England
Polly Stewart Fritch
1 Scott Lane
Greenwich, Conn. 06830

Chateau de la Napoule
Cannes, France

Le Cordon Bleu
24, rue du Champ de Mars
Paris 75007, France

École Nationale Supérieure de la
Pâtisserie
78, rue de la Croix-Nivert
Paris 75015, France

Paris en Cuisine
78, rue de la Croix-Nivert
Paris 75015, France

Giuliano Bugialli's Cooking in Florence
2830 Gordon Street
Allentown, Pa. 18104

Italianissimo
2708 East Franklin Street
Richmond, Va. 23223

La Varenne in Burgundy
Box 15313, Department 1B
Seattle, Wash. 98115

Hazan Classics
Box 285
Circleville, N.Y. 10919

L'École de Cuisine la Varenne
34, rue St. Dominique
Paris 75007, France

Princess Ere
2001, 18 avenue de la Motte-Picquet
Paris 75007, France

L'Académie du Vin
23 West Thirty-ninth Street
New York, N.Y. 10018

S. Lichine Tours International, Inc.
1 East Eighty-first Street
New York, N.Y. 10028

Sabine de Mirbeck École de Cuisine
Française
Clapham House
Litlington, East Sussex
BN26 5RQ, England

Catercall Cookery Courses
109 Stephendale Road
London, SW6 2PS, England

INDEX